DAVID McCOWEN
3652 Northlake Drive
Atlanta, Georgia 30340

CAIRO INTERNATIONAL EXHIBITION

FRANCO PURINI AND LAURA THERMES WITH DANIEL MODIGLIANI, PROJECT FOR THE ENLARGEMENT OF THE TOWN HALL OF CASTELFORTE, 1982-83, AERIAL PERSPECTIVE

Architectural Design Profile

CAIRO INTERNATIONAL EXHIBITION

MICHAEL GRAVES, VISUAL ARTS CENTRE, 1983

Guest-Edited by Jorge Glusberg

Jorge Glusberg Towards an Architectural Utopia **5**
Franco Purini & Laura Thermes Archaeological Excavations at Testaccio, Rome **7**
Michael Graves Center for the Visual Arts, Ohio State University **11**
Eisenman, Robertson Architects Firehouse for Engine Co 233, Ladder Co 176, Brooklyn **15**
Leon Krier The Reconstruction of the European City **17**
Herman Hertzberger Apollo Schools, Amsterdam **23**
Arata Isozaki Okanoyama Graphic Art Museum **27**
Philip Johnson & John Burgee AT&T Corporate Headquarters, NYC **31**
Josef Paul Kleihues Museum of Pre- and Early History at Frankfurt **33**
Richard Meier & Partners The High Museum of Art, Atlanta **36**
Christian de Portzamparc Conservatory of Music and Retirement Home, Paris **41**
Henri Ciriani Archaeological Museum at Arles **45**
Vittorio Gregotti & Gino Pollini Science Department at the University of Palermo **49**
Rob Krier Houses 7 & 16, Block 31, Linden-/Ritterstrasse, West Berlin **52**
Moore Ruble Yudell Parish of St Matthew Episcopal Church, Ca **53**
Hans Hollein Kulturforum, West Berlin **57**
Alvaro Siza Avelino Duarte House, near Ovar **61**
James Stirling, Michael Wilford & Associates Cornell University Performing Arts Center **63**
Miguel Angel Roca Projects for the City of Cordoba, Argentina **66**
Robert A M Stern Residence at Chilmark, Martha's Vineyard **71**
Tigerman Fugman McCurry Knoll International Showroom at Houston **73**
Mario Botta One-Family House at Morbio Superiore **77**
Aldo & Hannie Van Eyck Restaurant and Conference Facilities for ESTEC, Noordwijk **80**
O M Ungers Museum of Architecture at Frankfurt **85**
John Hejduk Three Projects **86**

JACQUES BEDEL, LUIS F BENEDIT, CLORINDO TESTA, CULTURAL CENTRE FOR THE CITY OF BUENOS AIRES, 1979

Editor: Dr. Andreas Papadakis

First published in Great Britain in 1984 by Architectural Design
AD Editions, 7 Holland Street, London W8

Copyright © 1984 AD Editions *All rights reserved*
The entire contents of this publication are copyright and cannot be reproduced in any manner whatsoever without written permission from the publishers

AD Profile 56 is published as part of Architectural Design Volume 54 11/12-1984

Distributed in the United States of America by
St Martin's Press, 175 Fifth Avenue, New York, NY 10010

Library of Congress Catalog Card No 84-52472
ISBN 0-312-82780-6 (USA)
ISBN 0-85670-852-6 (UK)

Printed in Great Britain by E.G. Bond Ltd., London

JORGE GLUSBERG
Towards an Architectural Utopia

The International Union of Architects (UIA) is more than thirty-five years old. It was founded in 1948, when reconstruction was the order of the day, to bring together architects from all countries without any distinction as to nationality, race, religion, politics, architectural doctrine or local architectural standards.

The goal was to link the various national architectural organisations by each member of one organisation becoming a member of the UIA, thereby enjoying all the benefits of membership of the UIA and closer links with his colleagues from other countries. This has certainly been achieved: today the UIA has ninety-three National Sections and a membership of some one million architects. The UIA has become one of the most comprehensive and most effectively organised non-governmental bodies maintaining close links with the major intergovernmental agencies.

Besides representing architects and promoting the different areas of architecture (national development, town planning, programming and management, industrial design, crafts and interior design), the UIA has also been a forum for discussion, providing opportunities for study, research and the exchange of new ideas and information. It has promoted and disseminated culture, in the broader and only true meaning of the word, namely culture which is not limited to the arts, thought, science and technology, but takes in all the forms of creative social activity and the development of the civic and political life of society. In short, it has become a major force in the struggle to improve the quality of life and foster respect for human dignity.

Despite these achievements, the UIA still needed to develop a clearer and more decisive approach to the problems of society at large. It had to take a step forward so that the gains and advances of the past thirty-five years would be consolidated in a body concerned with giving leadership and a sense of direction to present and future generations, in an association of specialists committed to playing a part in shaping the new civilisation awaited by man. The UIA therefore found itself faced with the task of adapting from within to the new developments in society and meeting the demands and claims of a world whose problems would be unbearable without its hopes. While not all members of society are architects, no architect can escape being a member of society. While no specific form of democracy corresponds to a particular architectural style, no architectural style that fails to reflect democratic values can claim to be true architecture. While high culture is a whim of intellectual elites and a farce for dictators, culture is an essential element in the sovereignty of each people in the concert of nations.

One of America's great writers, the Dominican Pedro Henriquez Ureña, declared: 'The ideal of justice takes precedence over the ideal of culture; a passion for justice is nobler than the quest for intellectual perfection. The self-centred dilettantism of Leonardo and Goethe stands in contast with the single-mindedness of Plato, our first master of utopia, who burnt all his poetic works to preach truth and justice in in the name of Socrates, whose death brought home to him the frightening imperfection of the society in which he lived'.

The key word in this quotation is 'utopia'. We tend to think of utopia as something illusory or unattainable. Nothing could be farther from the truth. The idea of utopia has always been underpinned by a recognition of the value of human effort directed to the improvement of the individual and collective lives of men and women here and now. The Renaissance period, when the idea of utopia flourished again, was essentially utopian. Since then, the idea of utopia has been eclipsed but has never disappeared completely. Could not the ecology movement be described as utopian?

The UIA found itself faced with the task of helping to create the utopia needed by today's world. It recognised the necessity of bringing about an architectural utopia, thereby making a positive contribution to the permanent integration of architecture in the construction of societies that are freer and fairer, that is to say, societies marked by greater humanity, greater harmony and a greater sense of justice.

The UIA has now set out on this path.

The turning-point in the UIA's history was the XVth Assembly of the Union, which took place in the Polish city of Katovice, during the course of the XIVth UIA World Congress in Warsaw.

The Assembly is the supreme body of the UIA. It is made up of delegations from all the National Sections. Every three years it meets to set out the policy and programme of the UIA and appoint the members of its governing bodies (the Board and the Bureau). At the XVth assembly, the Spanish architect Rafael de la Hoz was elected President. He and his fellow officers – the General Secretary, Michel Lanthonic (France); the treasurer, Charles-Edouard Geisendorf (Switzerland); and the Vice-Presidents Jerzy Buszkiewicz (Poland), Lington Loo (Malaysia), Padraig Murray (Ireland), Juan J Casal Rocco (Uruguay) and Yehua M Eid (Egypt) – were responsible for the 'Copernican' developments and far-reaching reforms that have taken place in recent years. Hoz has summed up these changes in the words: 'Democratisation, decentralisation and more effective communication'. The key concept underpinning the UIA's new role in relation to society at large is summed up in the theme of the XVth World Congress in Cairo: 'The mission of architecture in the society of today and the society of tomorrow'.

The Congress and Assembly in Cairo in January 1985 come three years after Poland. In my view, this has been one of the most significant periods in the history of the UIA. Its importance lies in the UIA's achievements, its current projects, its ever-stronger role as a guiding body and its success in communicating not just with its membership but with society at large and responding to the problems and needs of society.

The aim of the International Exhibition of Architecture, which coincides with the Congress and is featured in this special issue of *Architectural Design*, is to provide an initial synthesis of this current period in the life of the UIA. It does not mark the closing of a phase, for the UIA will certainly go on to consolidate and develop the approach that it has adopted. Rather, the aim of this exhibition is to summarise and symbolise – through the work of the leading architects who have agreed to take part – the key idea evolved and formulated by the UIA over the past three years; namely, the incorporation of the theory of 'architectural operators' into its approach to architecture.

The architects participating in the International Exhibition recognise the need to achieve, through the creation of effective 'architectural operators', a degree of harmonisation that conceals or diminishes the negative effect of buildings whose significance is at variance with their context and the network of social needs and functions and solutions which have to be proposed from the architectural and social points of view.

For this reason, we need to bear in mind the fact that the architect is not just a creator in his own specific field: he is also a link in a chain with many connections, all relating to the social advancement of human beings. Naturally, we are talking in terms of a humanistic architecture that reflects the ever varying requirements and needs both of man in society and of man and society. Man's values and interests should be the primary factors determining the complex network of social practices that include architecture.

Translated by Terence Lewis

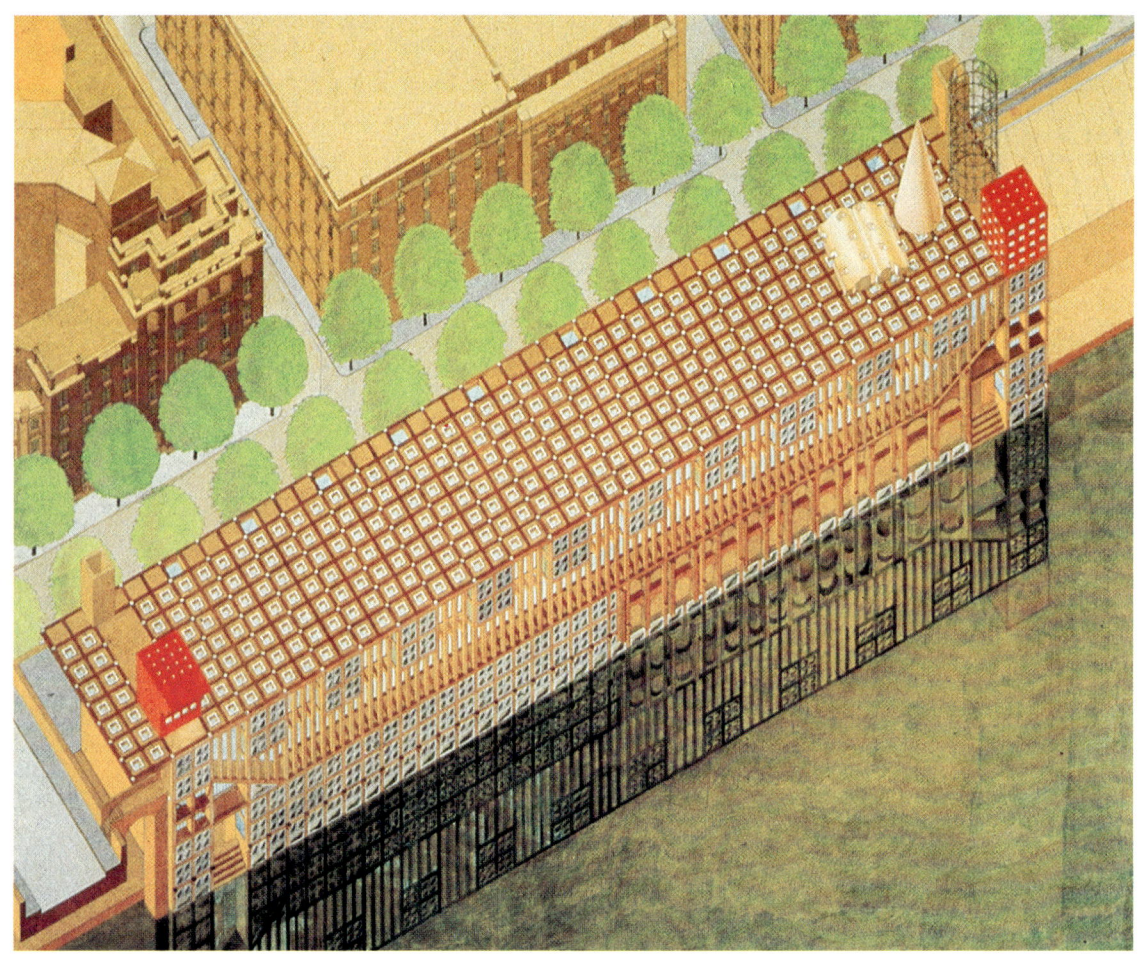

AXONOMETRIC, 3RD PHASE

PERSPECTIVE, 3RD PHASE

FRANCO PURINI & LAURA THERMES

Housing the archaeological excavations at the river port of Testaccio in Rome
1983

SECTIONAL PERSPECTIVE

The project was commissioned by the Archaeological Superintendency of Rome. Its theme is the protection of the remains of the Roman port on the Tiber in Rome's Testaccio district.

The proposal consists of a system to be achieved in three phases. In the first phase, a dam will be built to protect the excavations in case of flood. In the second phase, a roof will cover the excavation site from the dam to the river embankment. The roof covering will be made of large prefabricated beams in pre-stressed reinforced concrete, and as well as shielding the remains it will form an artificial base for the works relating to the third phase. In this last phase, a large rectangular pillared hall is planned. A wall running diagonally to the perimeter of the hall will divide it into a 'piazza' and separate smaller spaces for local activities. The hall could be built with the involvement of other boards besides the Archaeological Superintendency, which would already have achieved its aim of providing shelter for the port's remains with the completion of the second phase.

There are plans to transform the interior into a large public pool for the Testaccio district and other areas lacking amenities for swimming, boating and landing places on the river: this would put the Roman remains back in their original context. Besides providing a 150 × 20 m pool, gymnasiums, storage berths for rowing boats, dressing rooms, meeting rooms, a bar and a restaurant, the planned system would provide the surroundings for other activities linked with the district.

The image of a reconstructed 'natatio romana' (Roman swimming pool) is one potential of the Roman remains and the most authentic link to their original nature and role which, although lost today, is perhaps still renewable.

The project is in the shape of a large parallelogram formed by the repetition of a simple reinforced concrete trestle. Along the flank facing the river, rusticated tufa ashlar masonry surrounds a series of square apertures which illuminate the large pillared hall. The side facing the river is divided into three levels which correspond to the three phases of execution. The first consists of a dam and sluice with a series of moorings at the base. The second level consists of a two-level gallery which runs along the entire building and offers a view of the ruins as well as the river. The third is expressed in a '*redan*' movement alternately picked up by the pillars of the gallery and by the curtain wall.

Pure volumes – a cone, a cylinder and a cube – are placed on the roof covering to house the technical systems. A quotation from Le Corbusier, but also a reflection of the surrounding volumes of the Pyramid of Cestius and the gasometer, these objects appear on the roof, a geometric 'still life', almost as if it were the surface of a table. Situated at the other end of the 'table' towards the bridge is the custodian's house, a cube which portrays in frieze form a segment of the moulding.

A small bridge resting on an arch of the Sublico bridge links the gallery directly with the walking level of the bridge itself.

The succession of plans aims to assume in a progressive upward development the outline of the archeological findings as an 'intermittent' but recognisable memory. Although the ruins are not directly visible from the river and the embankment in front, and are in a sense negated by being 'imprisoned' within the large interior, the ruins are re-proposed and advanced directly up to the new water's edge by projecting their shape on the reinforced concrete trestle of the new structure.

In this way, a type of fade-in and fade-out is set up between the ancient outline and the new, between the constant rhythm of the new pillaring and the irregular rhythm of the ancient setting.

Collaborator: G. Neri.

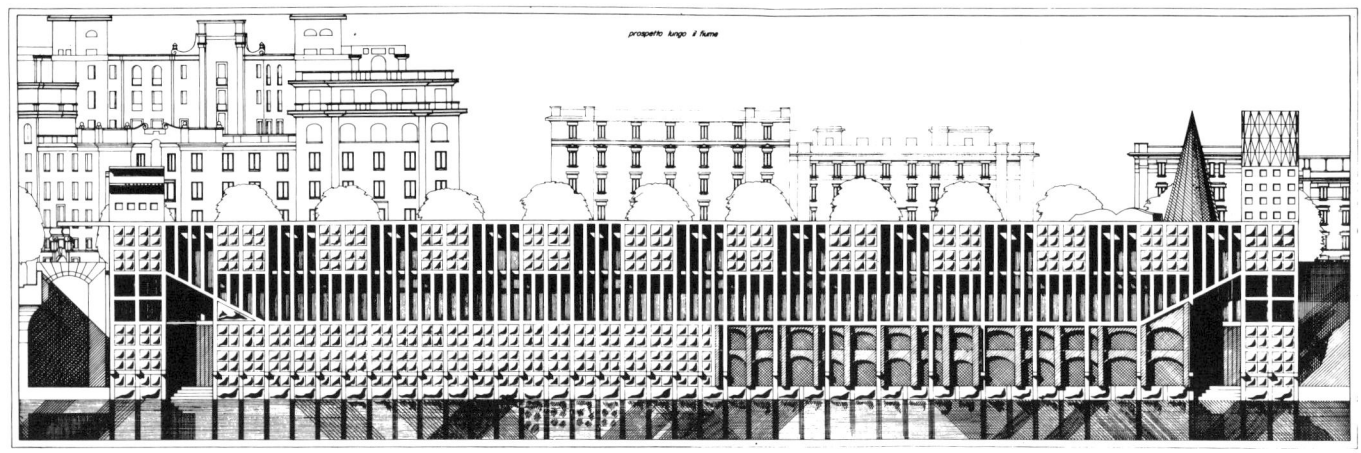
RIVER ELEVATION, 3RD PHASE

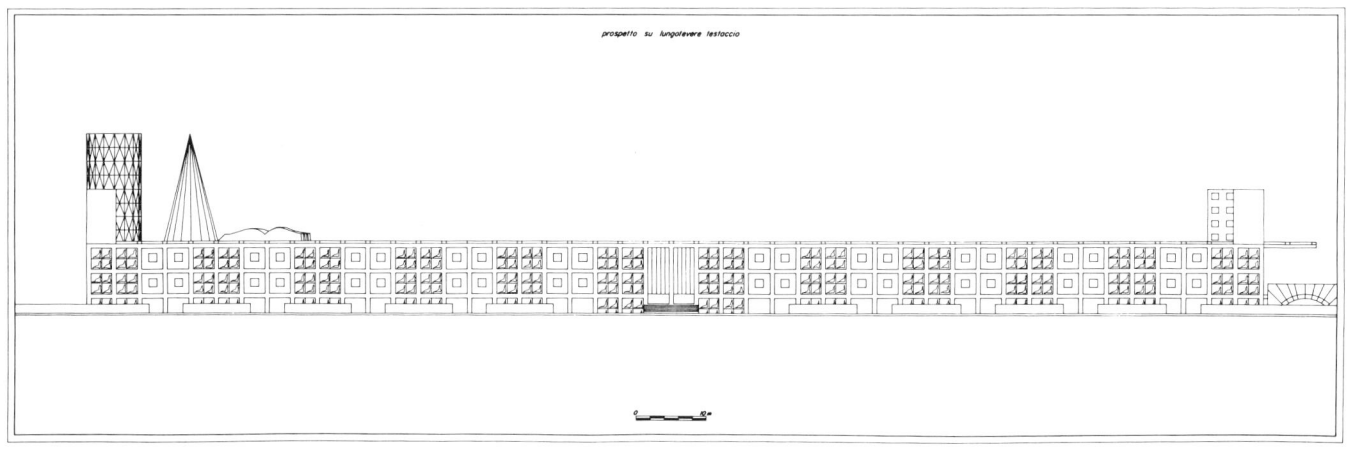
TESTACCIO ELEVATION, 3RD PHASE

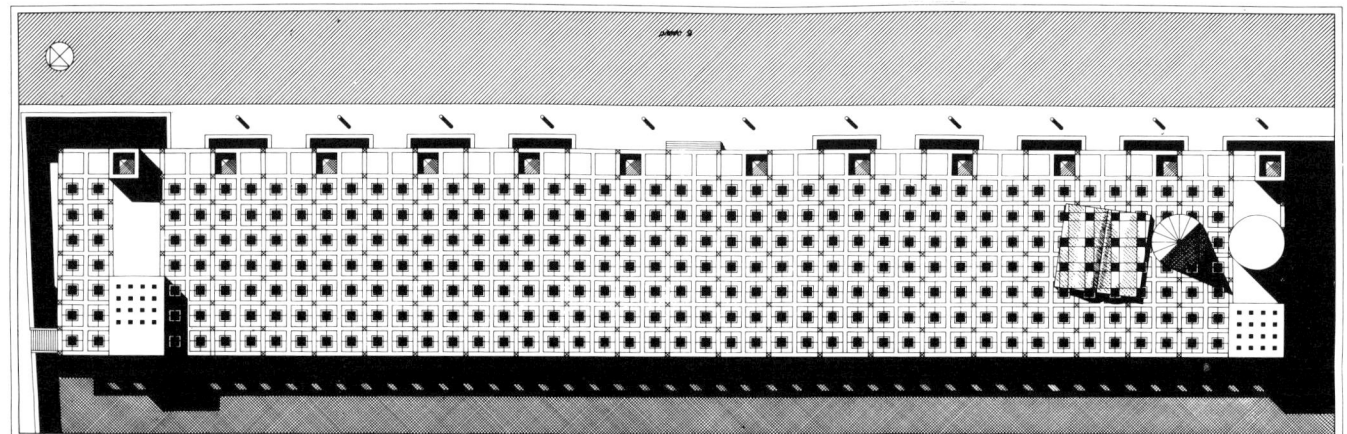
PLAN, 3RD PHASE

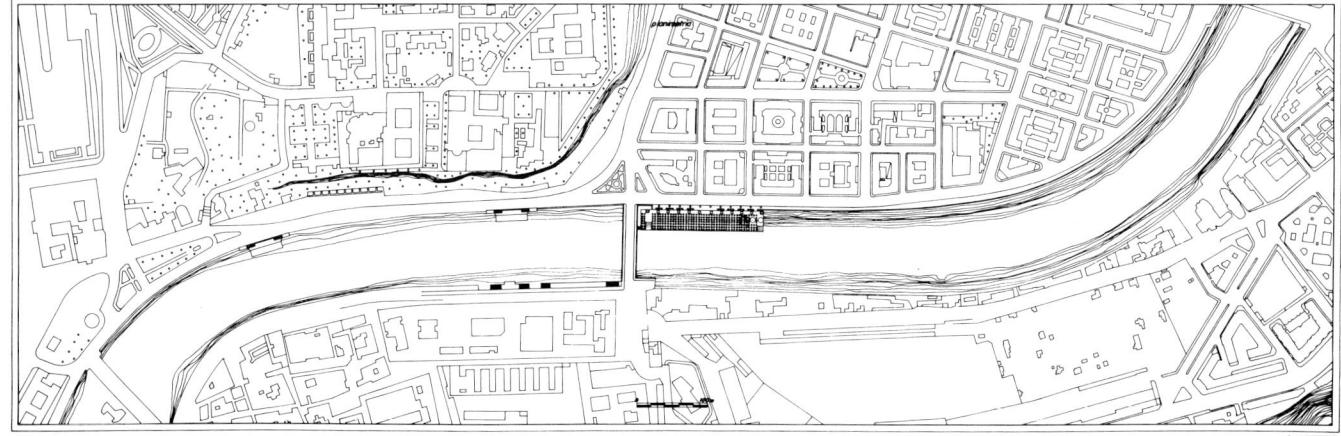
SITE PLAN, 3RD PHASE

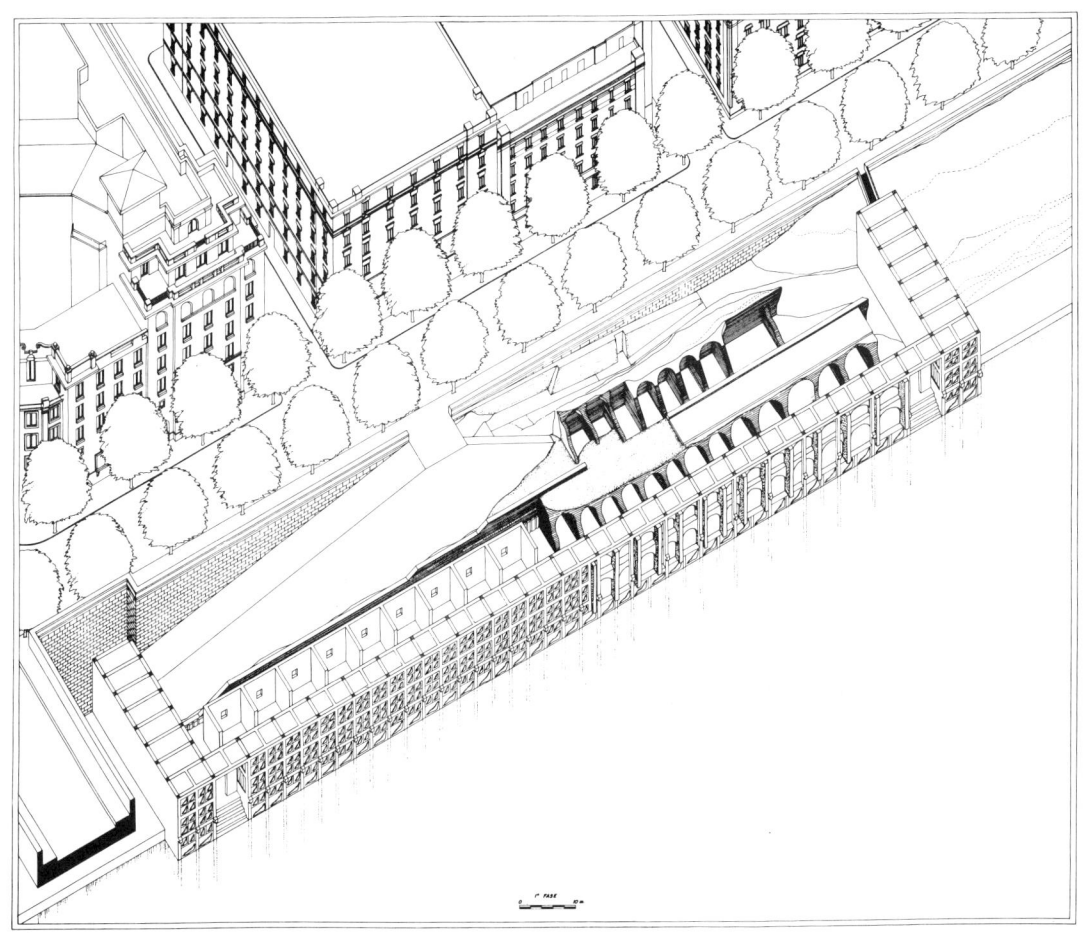
AXONOMETRIC, 1ST PHASE

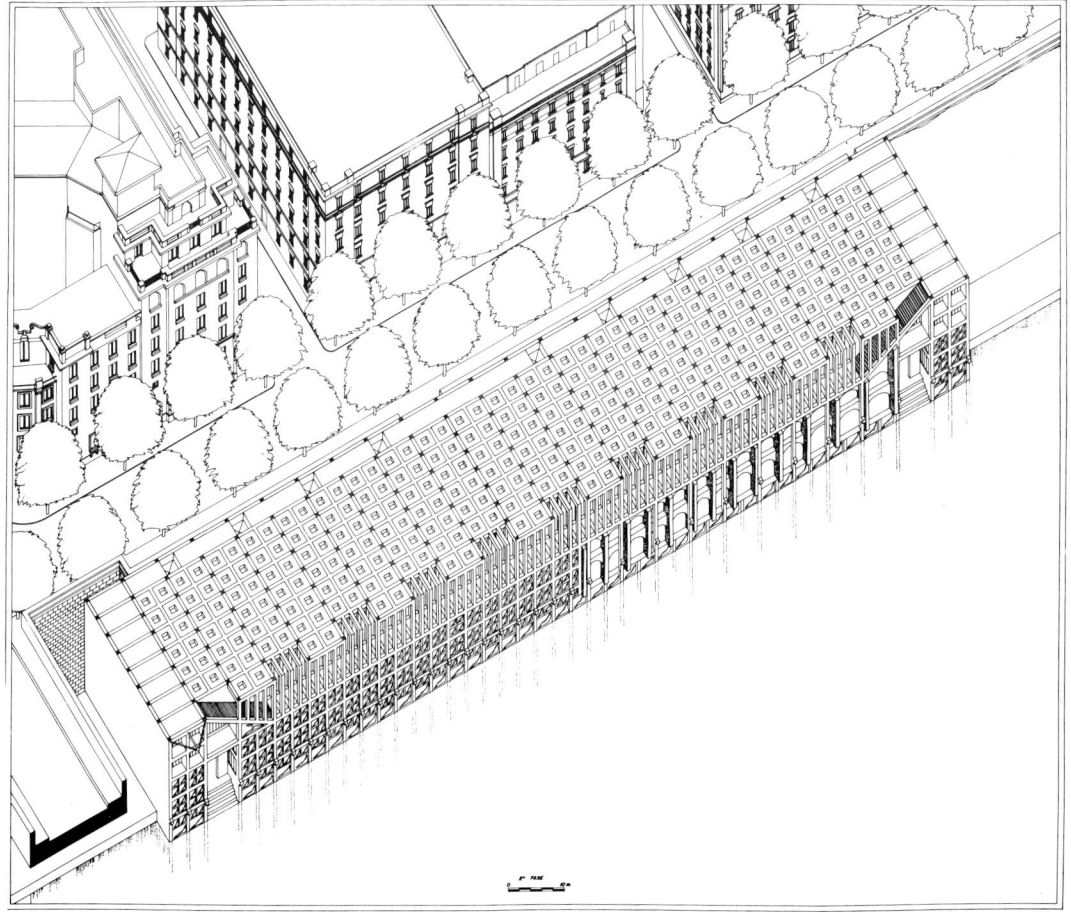
AXONOMETRIC, 2ND PHASE

COLLEGE ROAD ELEVATION

HIGH STREET ELEVATION

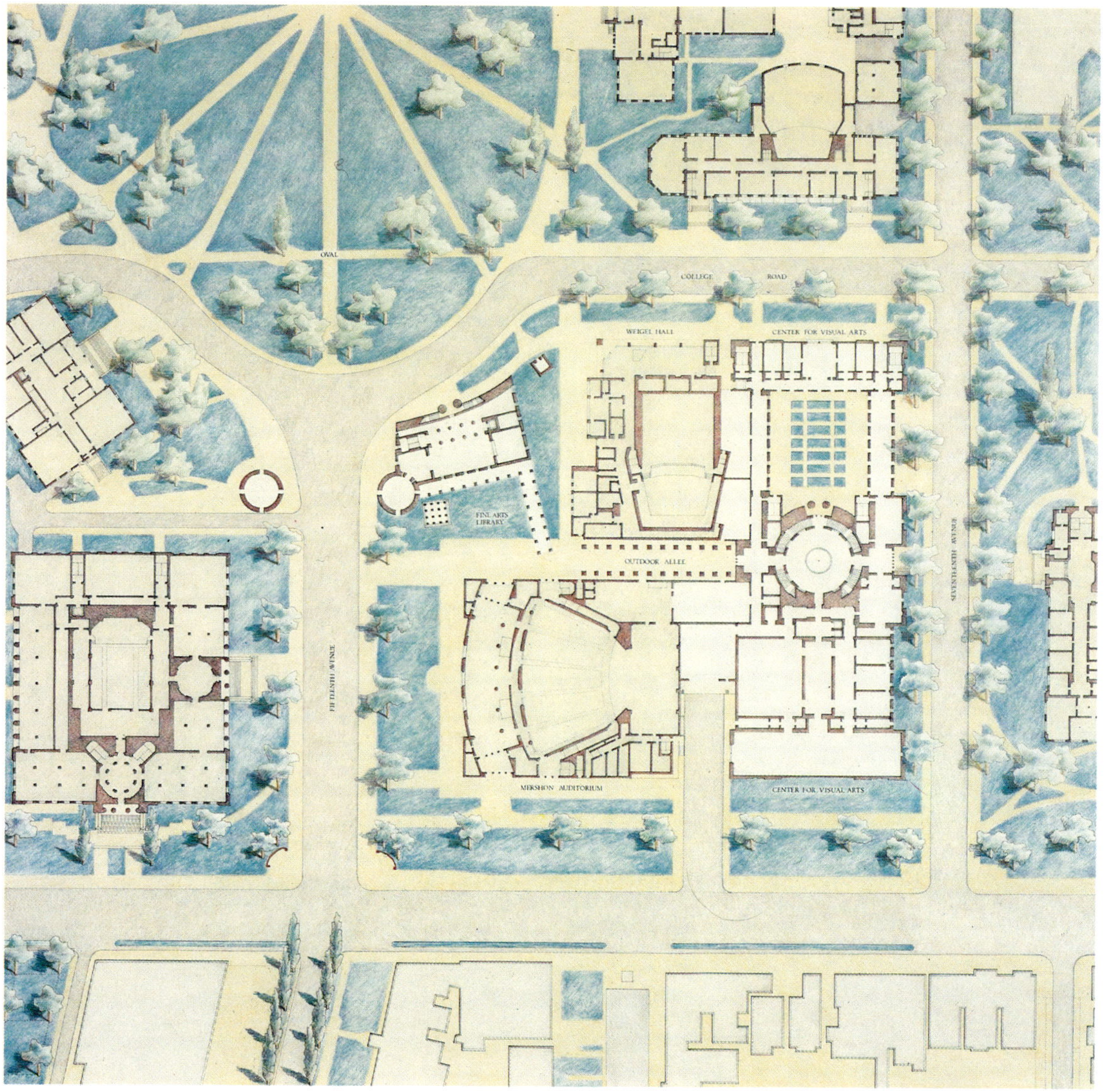

SITE PLAN

17TH AVENUE ELEVATION

MICHAEL GRAVES
Center for the Visual Arts, Ohio State University
Columbus, Ohio
1983

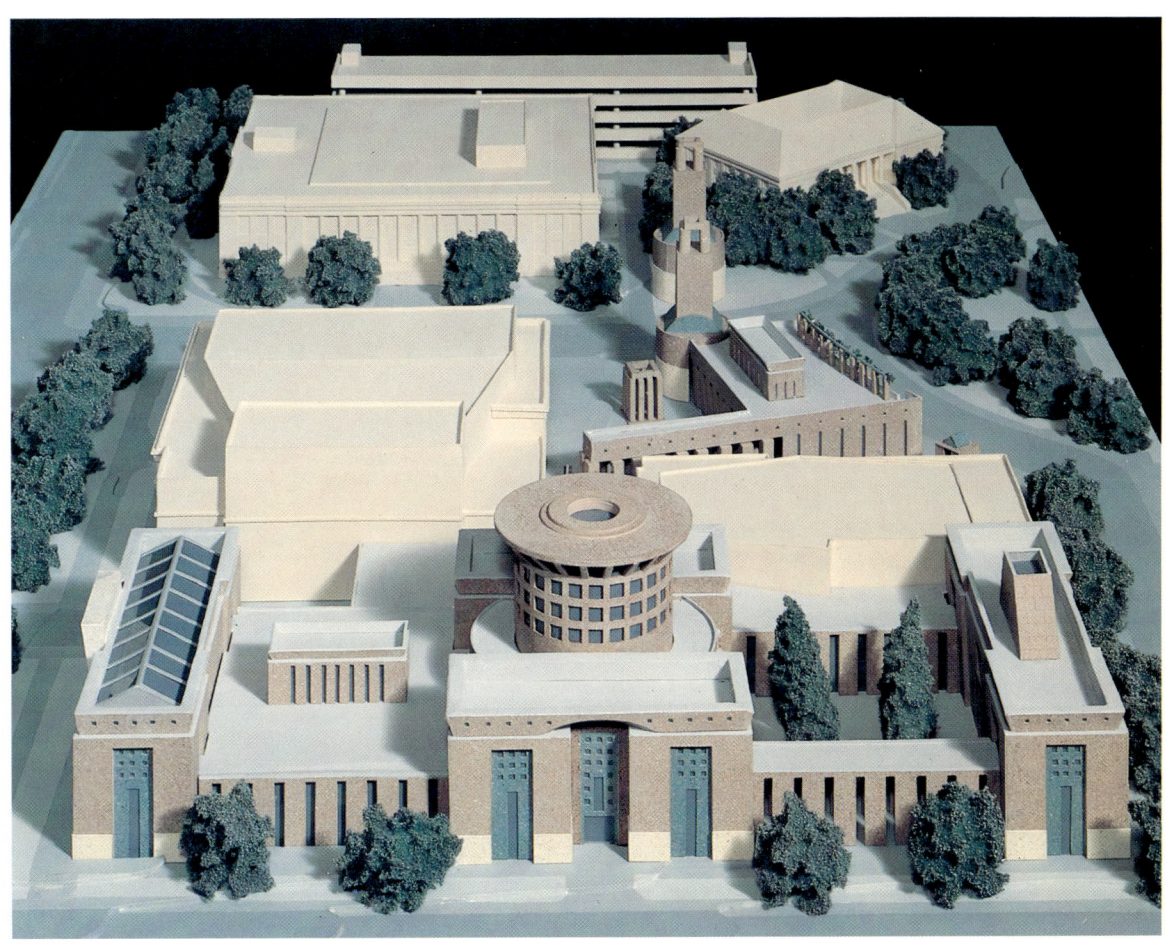

MODEL FROM 17TH AVENUE (PHOTO ACME PHOTO)

The design for the Center for the Visual Arts at Ohio State University allows the visitor to identify with, and orient to, the programmes held within. The major programmatic concerns are that the design accommodate the innovative and experimental nature of the university's visual arts programmes, and that the Center serve the public community as well as the campus community.

The proposed complex is sensitive to the existing structure of the campus. The 'Oval' is the focus of the site and the main circulation system of the campus. To enhance the importance of the Oval, two proposed pavilions serve as gates to the complex for the campus and the public. The siting of the complex reinforces existing vehicular and pedestrian traffic.

The Visual Arts Center is organised around a central rotunda (the 'Drum'), which is the formal, public entrance to the complex and a gathering place and place of visual orientation to the activities within the Center. The rotunda establishes a reciprocity between interior and exterior spaces and links the interior exhibition galleries to the east with the exterior exhibition court to the west. Second and third floor balconies in the rotunda overlook the lobby, extending further the public space. The second floor includes a restaurant with controlled views into the main and experimental galleries. This visual access allows interaction between the public and private areas without disrupting activity or security.

Compatible with the large exhibition scale, a second, smaller scale relates in detail to the human figure. The artists determine the character of their simple, flexible spaces for work, performance and exhibition.

The independent west wing houses the Institute for Advanced Study in the Visual Arts. This includes the fellows' studios (which are oriented to the campus Oval), the art and technology laboratory, a conference room and five seminar rooms. The laboratory is on the basement level with a double-height area open to the first floor.

The exhibition galleries and performance areas allow both traditional and developing forms of art; their sizes, proportions and equipment make possible new combinations of visual arts.

From the entrance rotunda, the visitor passes through an installation of the permanent collection. This helps establish an historical context for the large, temporary, topical shows in the main gallery and the advanced work planned for the experimental gallery.

The fine arts library occupies the northeast corner of the Oval and stands in the centre of the campus as a whole. Its autonomous position ensures security and greater accessibility to the arts community. Paired with the existing Page Hall, the library faces the Oval in the tradition of the surrounding buildings. One entry pavilion serves as an orientation area for the library, while the other is a campus information kiosk.

VIEW FROM 17TH AVENUE

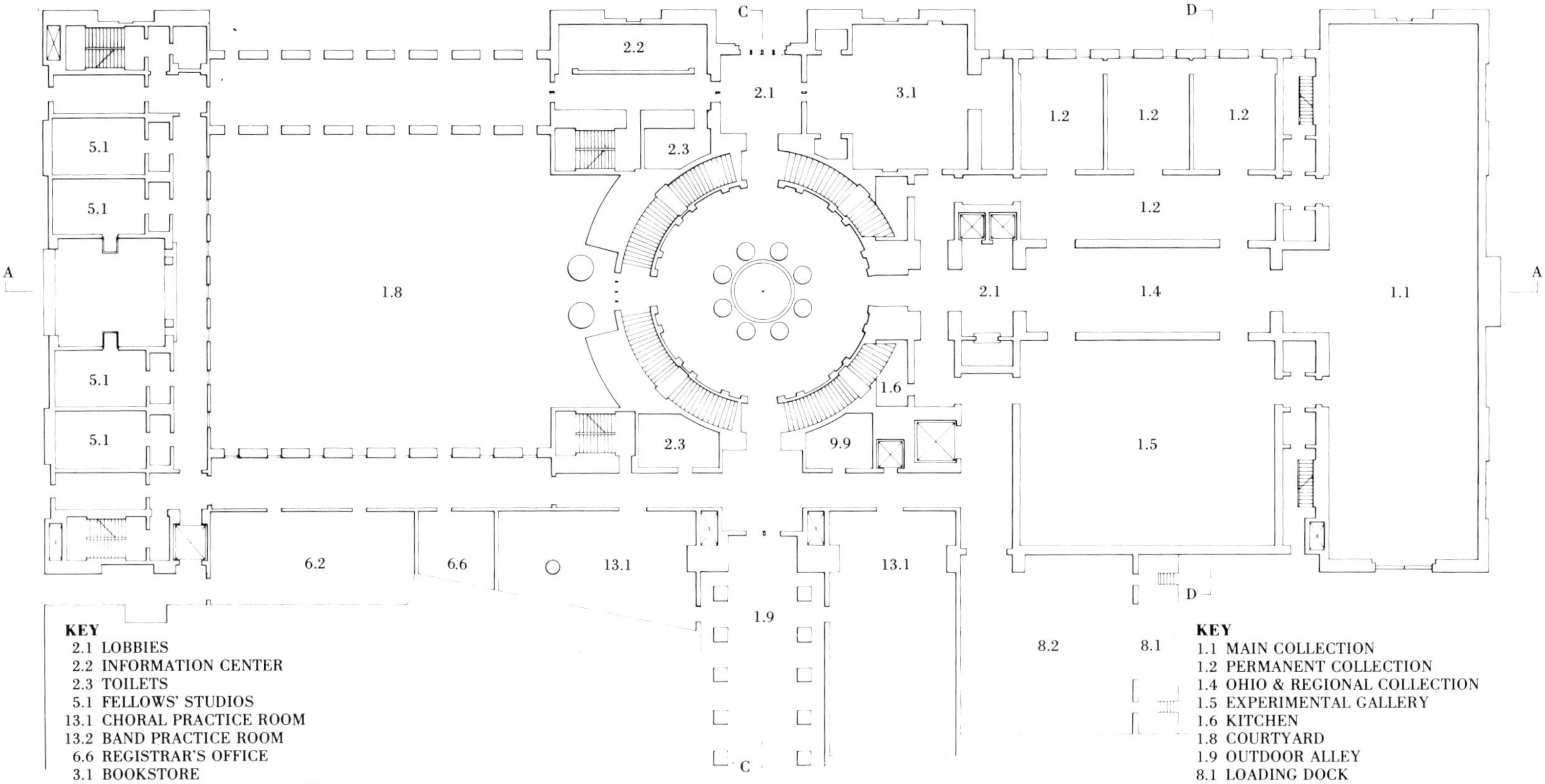

KEY
- 2.1 LOBBIES
- 2.2 INFORMATION CENTER
- 2.3 TOILETS
- 5.1 FELLOWS' STUDIOS
- 13.1 CHORAL PRACTICE ROOM
- 13.2 BAND PRACTICE ROOM
- 6.6 REGISTRAR'S OFFICE
- 3.1 BOOKSTORE
- 6.2 ELECTRONIC ACCESS ROOM

KEY
- 1.1 MAIN COLLECTION
- 1.2 PERMANENT COLLECTION
- 1.4 OHIO & REGIONAL COLLECTION
- 1.5 EXPERIMENTAL GALLERY
- 1.6 KITCHEN
- 1.8 COURTYARD
- 1.9 OUTDOOR ALLEY
- 8.1 LOADING DOCK
- 8.2 SHIPPING & RECEIVING

FIRST FLOOR PLAN

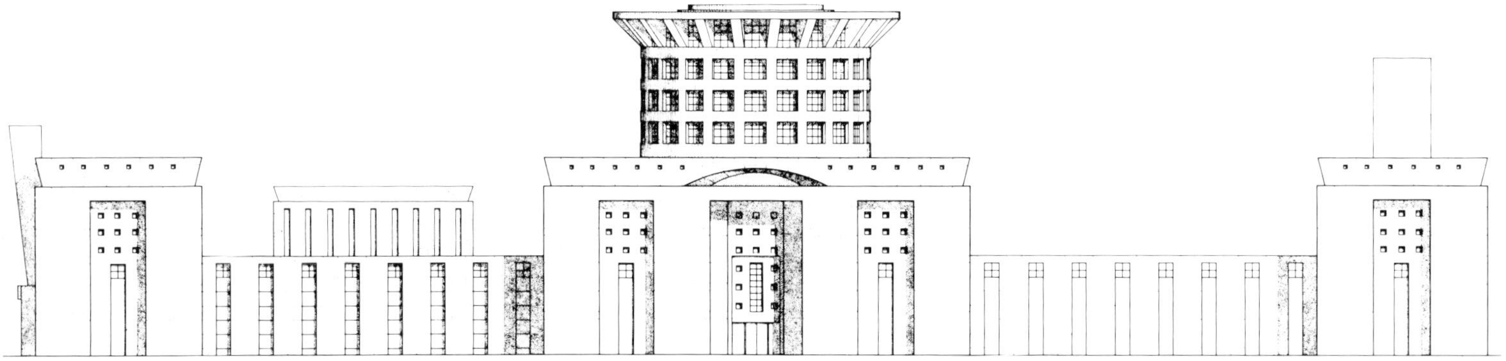

17TH AVENUE ELEVATION

12

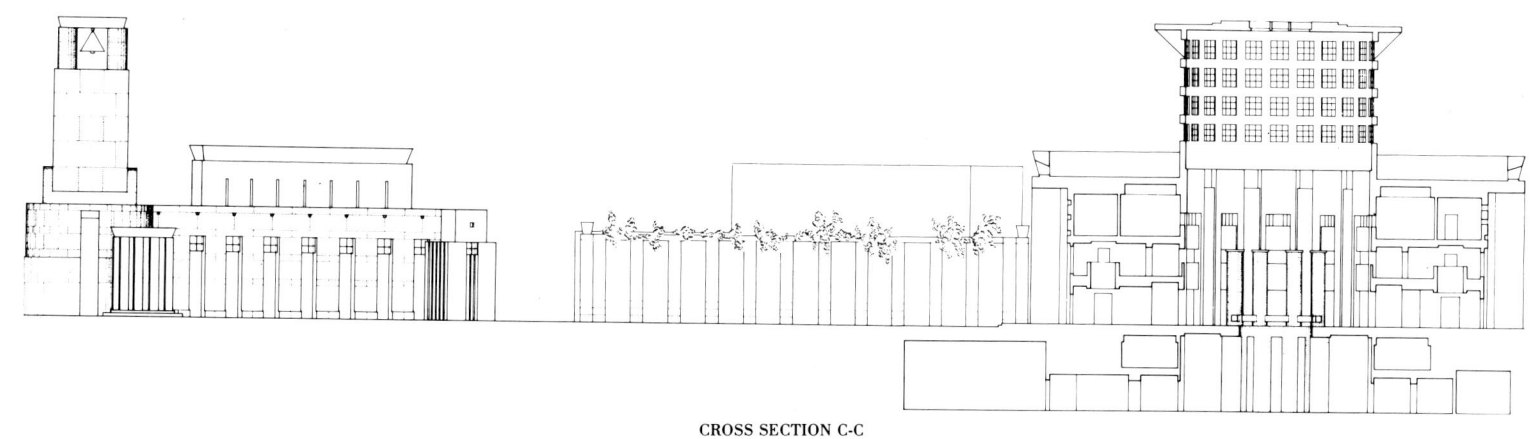
CROSS SECTION C-C

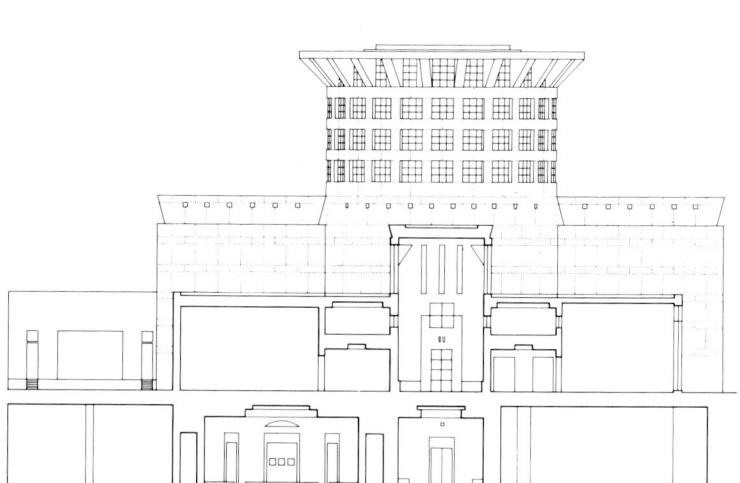
CROSS SECTION D-D

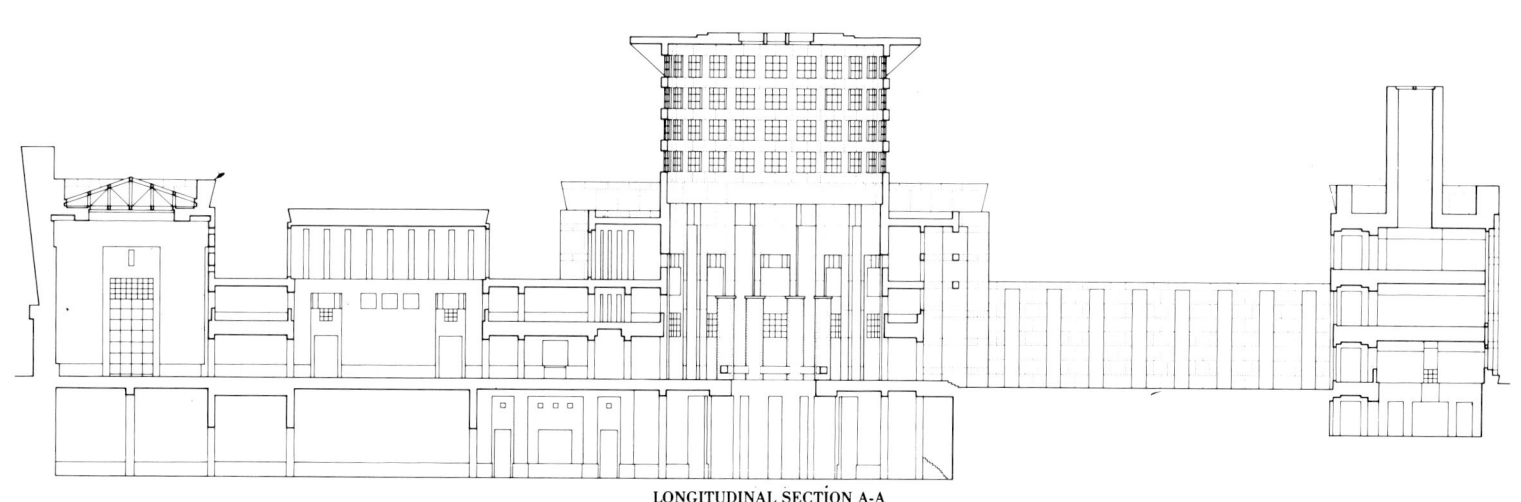
LONGITUDINAL SECTION A-A

PERSPECTIVE FROM SOUTH-WEST CORNER

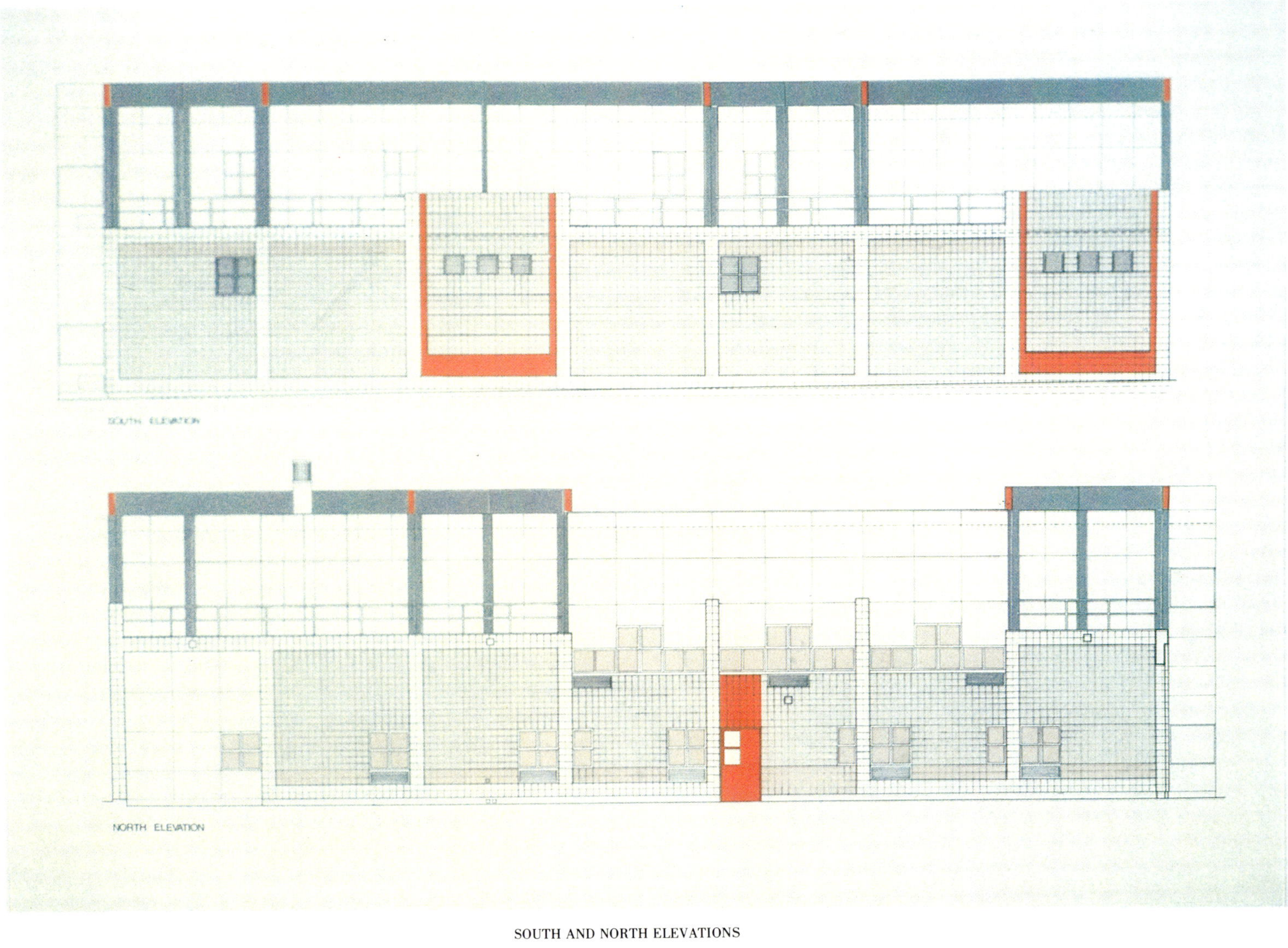

SOUTH AND NORTH ELEVATIONS

EISENMAN ROBERTSON ARCHITECTS
Firehouse for Engine Company 233, Ladder Company 176
1984

This project for a fire station in an area of Brooklyn undergoing revitalisation is intended as a public marker, a 'literal beacon' of unity on a site which is roughly divided by two different grid contexts and a major elevated mass-transit line marking the east-west division of those grids. The building, which houses both a battalion chief and a ladder company, attempts another kind of urban marking within its own form rather than the present-day imagery dealing with contextualism and historicism. Here, the imagery of the building does not refer outside itself to pop super-graphics and classical pastiche. Rather, the imagery of the building *is* the meaning of the site: it creates a union of the two grids by superimposing the geometry of the northern grid (recalling the masonry scale of the existing context). The roof members of the superimposed grid contain red laser lights, and the beam ends contain a beam of light so that at night the structure is symbolically illuminated and can be seen from passing trains as well as the street. When the engines are out at a fire, the beam ends send out a beacon of red light to complete the imagery of the project.

Collaborators: Peter Eisenman (Design Partner); Arthur Baker (Partner-in-Charge); Ross Woolley (Project Architect); Mark Wamble, David Winslow (Assistants); John Altieri (Mechanical and Electrical Engineers); Robert Silman Associates (Structural Engineers); Robert Slutzky (Artist)

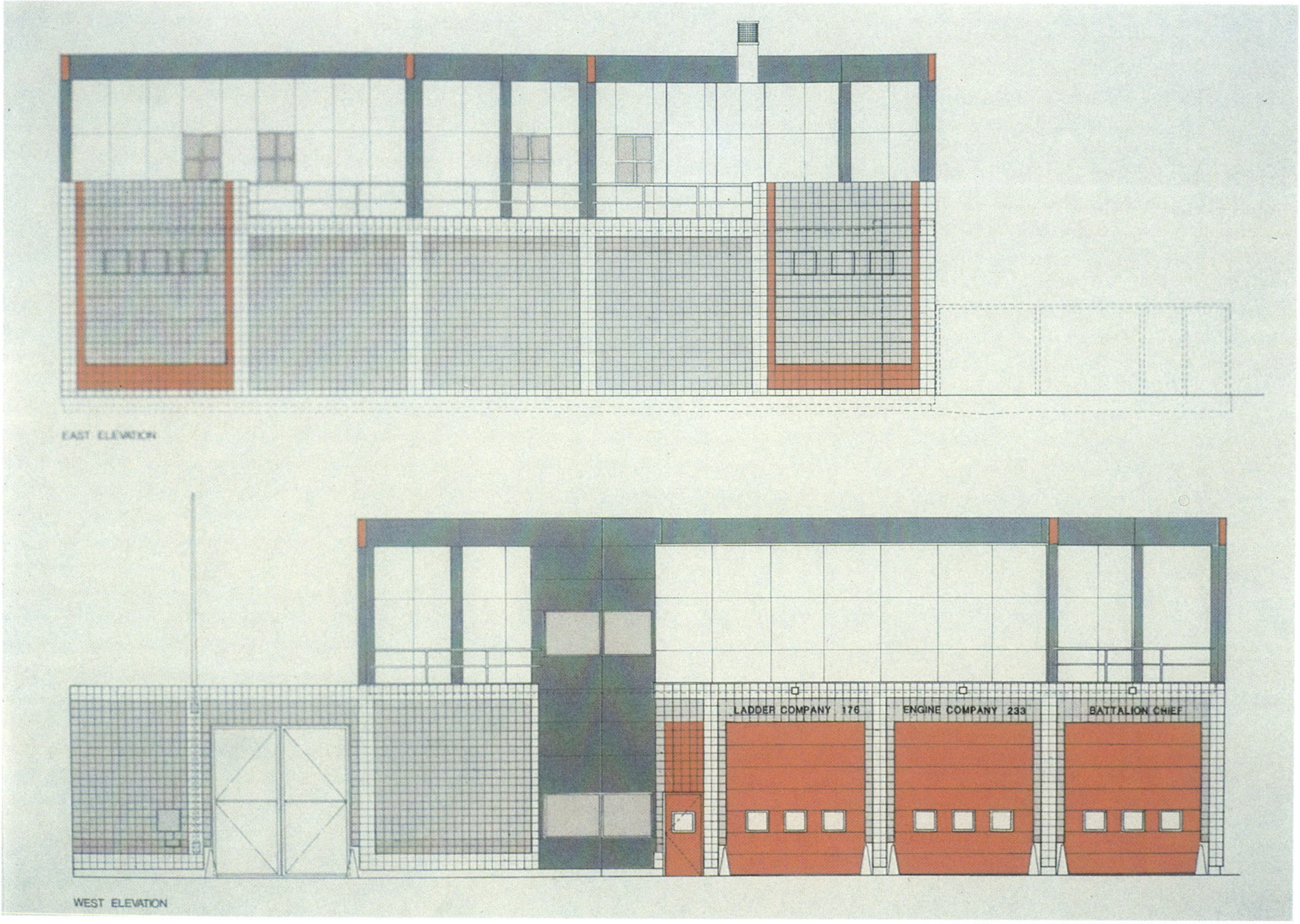

MODEL

EAST AND WEST ELEVATIONS

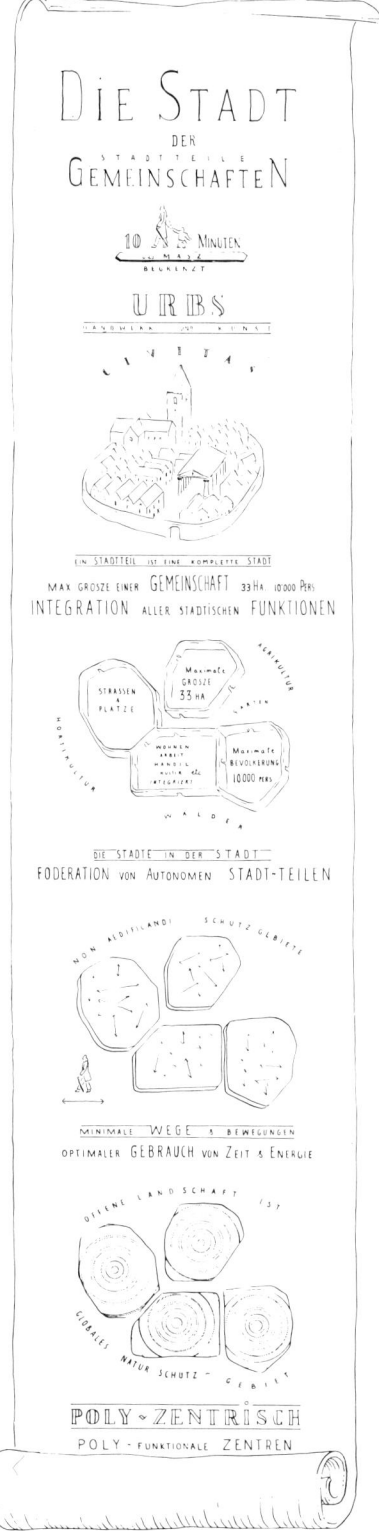

THE ANTI-CITY OF FUNCTIONAL ZONES	THE CITY OF QUARTERS COMMUNITIES
UNLIMITED	THE MEASURE LIMITED
	CRAFTS AND ARTS
MASS-SOCIETIES	A QUARTER IS A COMPLETE CITY
NEITHER CITY NOR LANDSCAPE	MAX SIZE OF A COMMUNITY = 33 HA 10,000 PEOPLE
	INTEGRATION OF ALL URBAN FUNCTIONS
OBLIGATORY SEGREGATION OF DAILY URBAN FUNCTIONS	A CITY WITHIN THE CITY FEDERATION OF AUTONOMOUS QUARTERS
	PROTECTED AREAS
MAXIMUM DISTANCES AND MOVEMENTS	MINIMAL DISTANCES AND MOVEMENTS
MAXIMUM CONSUMPTION OF TIME AND ENERGY	OPTIMAL USE OF TIME AND ENERGY
	OPEN LANDSCAPE IS A
NIGHT DAY	GLOBAL NATURE PROTECTION AREA
A-CENTRIC MONO-FUNCTIONAL "CENTRES"	POLY-CENTRIC POLY-FUNCTIONAL CENTRES

THE RECONSTRUCTION OF THE EUROPEAN CITY

An Outline for a Charter*

LEON KRIER

A CHARTER FOR THE RECONSTRUCTION OF the City is the necessary complement to a charter for the Reconstruction of the Countryside. They can both only be built upon a *long-term political and ecological CONSENSUS.* They must transcend the limited interests of political, industrial and financial organisations and of cultural and religious groups. A charter is a global moral project which describes the rights and duties of the individual and of societies. It is the mirror image and necessary complement of a political constitution of a people.

I CRITIQUE OF INDUSTRIAL RATIONALITY:
Development and Progress
The myth of unlimited technical progress and industrial development has brought the most 'advanced' countries to the brink of ecological exhaustion. Industrial forms of production, that is, the extreme development of productive means and forces, have destroyed in less than 200 years the cultures and traditions, landscapes and cities which had been the culmination of centuries of human experience and inventiveness, of skill and intelligence; they now erode the very resources and the fundamental human values without which mankind can neither live nor survive.

Industrial Planning and Functional Zoning
Industrial development is effected through the fragmentation of integrated and polyfunctional rural and urban complexes (cities, villages, districts, quarters, parishes) into monofunctional sub-urban zones (residential neighbourhoods, university campuses, shopping centres, industrial parks etc . . .).
– Monofunctional zoning (productive, commercial, administrative, educational, residential, recreational) is the technical instrument of this fragmentation.
– Monofunctional programming and the privileged allocation of financial resources to such programmes are its political and economic motor.

Against the organic integration of urban functions, industrial zoning posits their mechanical segregation.

*Note: this text is based on an outline written in 1978.

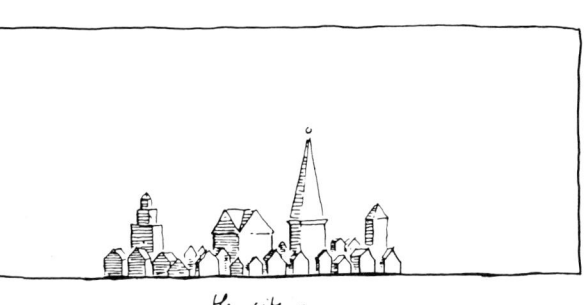

the city

the Anti-City

Imperatives of Functional Zoning
1. The first imperative of zoning is to transform any part of the territory (city and countryside) in such a way that every citizen can only perform:
– one function
– in one place
– at one time

at the exclusion of all other functions.

2. The second imperative of zoning is the effective and daily *mobilisation* of industrial society in its entirety (all classes, all ages, all species, all races; adults, old people, children, rich and poor, employers and employed, unemployed and misers) in order to perform even the simplest functions of life.

Consequences of Functional Zoning
The most remarkable consequence of functional zoning is that it guarantees the *maximum consumption* of units of time, energy and hardware per and in between the accomplishment of all major and minor urban functions.

– *Circulation* of people, hardware and information are the principal activities to be generated by the industrial metabolism of man and nature.

– Roads, railways, canals, airstrips, cables, pipelines, etc, are the arterial system of an atomised society, its paradoxical common place.

– The train, the car, the plane, the computer, the telephone and television are its principal instruments, the necessary extensions of the human body and mind.

Politics of Industrial Zoning
– All industrial states, independently of their political ideologies, promote and where necessary impose the functional zoning of cities and countryside against all forms of resistance.

– Functional zoning is not a neutral technical planning instrument; it is the means to destroy the infinitely complex cultural and economic fabric of urban life, culture and democracy, of communities which by nature are based on artisanal modes of production, trade and communication.

– Against the organic order of the city, functional zoning establishes the mechanical disorder of the anti-city.

– The functional fragmentation of the city results *ipso facto* in the destruction of the countryside; it means the effective dissolution of both the idea of countryside and of city; it reduces rural and urban communities, landscapes and forests, nature and artifacts, to mere statistical entities, expressed in exchangeable numbers and densities.

– Industrial rationality conflicts with and contradicts social, ecological, ethical and aesthetic rationality. It transforms every citizen into a potential and involuntary agent of energy waste.

– Industrial rationality means the effective suspension of the idea of economy and morality. Its achievement is the creation of social and ecological problems and disasters which it is unable and unwilling to avoid, to resolve and hence to take responsibility for or think about. It suspends the notion of individual or collective responsibility for its own goals and ends.

– Industrial rationality is by nature amoral, asocial, and anti-ecological; it is both the *instrument* and the *expression* of moral, ecological and social irrationality and collapse.

– No form of industrial planning or planned industrial economy, neither *private* nor *public* transport policies can effectively curtail the waste of material and human energy resources caused by Functional Zoning, by the industrial anti-city.

II A GLOBAL PROJECT FOR THE RECONSTRUCTION OF THE CITY:
An Ecological Project

The global destruction of cities and countryside, of human cultures and nature itself can only be reversed by a global philosophical, technical, cultural, moral and economic project; by an ECOLOGICAL project.

The city is not the necessary and unavoidable result of a society's activities. It can only be built and maintained when it represents the highest possible goal of individuals, of a society and of its institutions. A city is not a mere economic accident but a moral project.

Not the forms of production but the form of the city itself must dictate the organic nature and moral order of the city, qualifying and shaping the forms of production and exchange.

The Nature of the City
– City and Countryside are antithetical notions.

– Like all organisms in nature, a city must be a finite object; it has a mature, ie a maximum and a minimum size, both in surface and volume, in plan and silhouette, in the number of inhabitants it can house and in the number of activities it can allow and perform.

– Just like a mature individual, a mature city can be neither enlarged nor expanded in any direction; just like a family of individuals it can only grow by multiplication.

– Contradicting and in contrast to the a-centrality and functional monotony of industrial zones, a city is a geographical centre of limited size, integrating all periodic and a-periodic urban activities, functions and uses, whether private or public, commercial or productive, religious and political in nature.

– A *metropolis* is formed by a smaller or greater number of independent and autonomous cities, by a federation of cities. The *metropolis* provides for those functions of national and international importance which overburden and overcrowd the daily lives of one single city. These activities are located the malls and parks, along the avenues and squares which separate the different cities of a metropolitan federation, or alternatively along the parades and boulevards which form its boundaries and limits towards the countryside. The *metropolis* must have a centre and a well-defined, readable limit.

– A *city* is formed by a maximum of four urban quarters. It provides for periodic and a-periodic functions of regional importance which would overburden and overcrowd the daily working of one single quarter. These activities are located within the avenues and squares which separate the different quarters or, alternatively, along the boulevards which form the boundary and limits of the *city* and its quarters. The *city* must have a centre and a well-defined, readable limit.

– The urban *quarter* is a true city within the city. As a part, it contains the features and qualities of the whole. It is a full and mature member of the family of quarters which form the city. The urban quarter provides for all periodic local (daily and weekly) urban functions (residential, educational, productive, administrative, commercial, recreational, etc) within a limited piece of land dimensioned on the comfort of a walking man, not exceeding 33 hectares in surface and 15,000 inhabitants in population. A quarter must have a centre and a well-defined, readable limit.

The Walking Man
The walking man should be able to reach on foot, and without the use of mechanical means of transport, all habitual daily and weekly functions within a maximum of 10 minutes walk. Such an area measures approximately 33 hectares. Fatigue sets the natural limit to what a human being is prepared to walk daily, and this limit has taught men through history the size of comfortable rural and urban communities.

There seems, however, to be no natural limit to the size of a functional zone, nor to that of the industrial Anti-City. The boredom which befalls man when using mechanical means of transport (public or private) teaches him nothing but makes him instead forget his sense of limit in time and space.

In a metropolitan federation of independent cities the importance of mechanical means of transport, whether public or private, will be greatly reduced; they will serve principally a-periodic needs and they will become instruments of privilege and pleasure.

The Form of Urban Spaces
The form of the city and of its public spaces cannot be a matter of personal experiment. Public spaces can only be built in the form of streets (linear spaces) and squares (nodal spaces). Whether of grand metropolitan or intimate local quality, they must present a permanent and familiar character, their dimensions and proportions obtained from and verified by a millenary culture of *streets* and *squares*.

Strategy and Tactics of Reconstruction
– Immediate cancellation and total revision of existing planning statutes and procedures;
– cancellation and prohibition of any kind of functional surface zoning;
– drastic reduction of the total urban land;
– drastic extension of the NON AEDIFICANDI zones, coinciding with the notion of nature conservation areas;
– all extra – urban land, whether of sylvicultural, horticultural or agricultural use, will become integral parts of nature conservation areas.
– Building structures situated outside the new urban perimeters will only be for agricultural, sylvicultural or horticultural uses.
– Large-scale industrial complexes will be prohibited.
– Existing large-scale industrial, commercial, educational, culturally administrative, recreational etc complexes will be dissolved and rebuilt as limited urban units to be integrated within the perimeters of the metropolis, the cities or quarters, depending on their use and purpose.
– Small urban industries and artisanal workshops based on local employment will be systematically promoted, favouring as much as possible the creation and promotion of small economic circles of production and consumption and of supply and demand.
– Public transport (of people and wares) will be gradually de-subsidised, to become self-supporting after a 15-year period of urban reconstruction.
– Places of work, administration and commerce must be integrated with residences within a network of streets and squares; they must only occupy ground-floor and mezzanine levels through the entire city; conversely, no residences should be situated below the mezzanine levels. A vertical zoning of private and public functions will thus be promoted.
– Residential buildings and work premises will be situated principally on streets, courts, alleys, avenues and boulevards.
– Public and symbolic buildings (cultural, educational, recreational, religious) will be situated on public squares, in the visual focus of boulevards, avenues and streets.

– Public buildings will not be grouped but spread all over the urban quarters.
– All commercial, residential and industrial buildings lying outside the contracted urban perimeters will have to disappear within a period of 15 years.
– Their loss will be compensated by good urban land; the real estate value of these sites will in every case exceed that of the lost property and land.
– Ordinances concerning volumetric, constructional and stylistic proscriptions will be eased and promoted by generous tax privileges, reliefs and interest-free government loans.

Critique of the Industrialisation of Building
The industrialisation of building must be considered as a complete technical and political and cultural failure.

> Industrialisation has not brought any significant technical improvement in building.
> It has not reduced the cost of construction.
> It has not shortened the time of production.
> It has not created more jobs.
> It has not helped to improve the working conditions on the sites or in offices or workshops.
> It has on the contrary destroyed millenary and highly sophisticated crafts and arts.
> It has been incapable of finding solutions for the typological, social and morphological complexity of the historical centres and landscapes.

And although building is still today organised according to forms of artisanal production, craftsmanship as an autonomous culture has been destroyed by the industrial and social division of labour.
A culture of building and architecture must be based on a highly sophisticated artisanal and artistic tradition of construction.

Critique of Stylistic Pluralism
For the last two hundred years industrial states have disguised themselves in styles that have changed from generation to generation, nowadays from season to season. At first Neo-Classical then Neo-Gothic, then Modernist and now Kitsch triumphs from Las Vegas to Moscow and Peking.
Stylistic pluralism is by no means the sign of cultural prosperity, happiness, democracy and richness. It results from the confusion of artistic and industrial techniques. It results from the destruction of cultural traditions and ethnic identities. Cultural pluralism marks the moment where particular and private interests and obsessions replace a common and public culture.

The Use and Abuse of Architecture
There exists neither authoritarian nor democratic Architecture.

> There exists only authoritarian and democratic ways of producing and using architecture.
> A row of Doric columns is not more authoritarian than a tensile structure is democratic.
> Architecture is not political, it can only be used politically.
> Where architecture exists, it always transcends politics.
> Buildings can appear inhuman not through their Architecture but through their lack of Architecture.
> Buildings become inhuman when abstracted of architecture or dressed in false architecture.
> Kitsch is both abstraction and false appearance.
> There is neither reactionary nor revolutionary Architecture.
> There is only Architecture or its absence, that is, its abstraction.
> There has never been protest against Architecture.
> There has only been protest against the lack of Architecture, against its absence and ABSTRACTION.

Zeit-Geist and Zeit-Expression
It is impossible not to express in some measure the spirit of one's own time, and that is exactly what the notion Zeitgeist describes. Zeitgeist is as inescapable as body-smell, it is no guarantee of any kind of quality. Zeitgeist communicates itself despite ourselves. Zeitgeist can be of no concern to artists and craftsmen for they naturally long to attain a timeless quality using those materials, subjects and techniques which best resist the test of time, accident and taste. Buildings are not to be objects of immediate *consumption*. Buildings must be objects of long-term *use*.

Building and Architecture
Architecture can express nothing else but its own constructive logic, that is, its origin in the laws of building.
Building is the material culture of construction. As a craft, it is concerned with the construction of domestic structures, of workshops, of warehouses, of engineering works it is generally concerned with the erection of the urban fabric, of building blocks which form the streets of the city, its retaining walls, etc. Building culture is basically concerned with the repetition of a few building-types and the adaptation to local conditions of use, of materials and climate.
Architecture is the intellectual culture of building. As an art, it is concerned with the imitation and

translation of the elements of building into symbolic language, expressing in a fixed system of symbols and analogies the very origin of Architecture in the laws of building.

The very reason of Architecture to exist as a public Art is to attain to material and above all to intellectual permanence.

It can be no business of Architecture to express ever-changing functions or Zeitgeist.

Certain building types merely become associated with certain functions and celebrations and it is up to sculptural or pictorial iconography to help and sustain these associations.

Architecture is only concerned with the erection of public buildings and monuments, with the construction of public squares and sites.

Vernacular and Classical

Classical and Vernacular are cultures opposed to the production and consumption of futile objects.

Classical and Vernacular do not erect class distinctions but distinction between collective and individual, between monuments and urban fabric, public palace and domestic dwelling.

Classical and Vernacular cultures are based on the repetition of a few fundamental CONSTRUCTIVE AND FUNCTIONAL TYPES which are the universal expression of human activities of the Public, the Private and the Sacred.

Architecture and Building as Classical and Vernacular cultures are based on imitative systems of production, on artisanal tradition, where intellectual and manual faculties are exercised in harmony and not in conflict with each other.

In an artisanal culture, material or intellectual innovations become accepted only for their technical or artistic improvement and not as a result of a free-wheeling imagination. This process of slow and constant clarification and elaboration involves all the skills and intelligence of the individual artisan or artist.

Classical Architecture as the symbolic elaboration of vernacular building does not know INNOVATION as a virtue. It is fixed and immutable in its typological and morphological principles, but infinitely varied in its realisation, as are all objects of nature.

Architecture and Building are not objects of consumption. They can only be reconstructed in a perspective of material permanence as objects of use.

Without such permanence, without architecture transcending the lifespan of its builders, no public space, no collective expression as craft or art are ever possible.

Classical architecture and modernist* 'architecture' are contradictory, antagonistic and incompatible propositions – the former based on artisanal, artistic production; the latter on industrial modes of production.

The term classical denotes the best; it attains to the highest quality and belongs to artistic culture. The term industrial denotes the necessary; it attains to profitable quantity and belongs to material culture.

Transcending all questions of style, period and culture, classical architecture qualifies the totality of monumental architecture based on the fundamental principles of 'venustas, firmitas, utilitas', translated into modern language as harmony/beauty, stability/permanence and utility/comfort. These terms are unconditionally interdependent and their links have been exploded by all modernist 'architecture'.

The term architecture denotes the 'art of building' as an artistic culture of vernacular building. Vernacular building denotes the manual, artisanal culture of building based on tectonic logic.

The Domestic and the Monumental

It is only a dialogue of Architecture and Building, of Classical and Vernacular cultures, of monumental and domestic, of public and private that can endow human settlements with the dignity of a common culture.

Only a great functional complexity can lead to a rich, clear, permanently satisfying and beautiful articulation of the urban spaces and quarters.

Simplicity and legibility must be the goal of the very complexity of the urban plan and skyline silhouette.

A city articulated into
>public and domestic spaces
>monuments and urban fabric
>Architecture and building
>squares and streets
>>and in that HIERARCHY.

Criticism and Project

To protest against the transformation and destruction of the cities serves no purpose if we do not have a global alternative plan of reconstruction in our hands.

---

*Twentieth-century historians and critics endemically confuse the terms modern and modernist(ic). The term modern merely indicates period and time, whereas the term modernist(ic) has clear ideological and moral connotations. When historians write about 'the Modern Movement' they clearly mean by this term 'the modernist movements' as opposed to 'the traditionalist movements'.

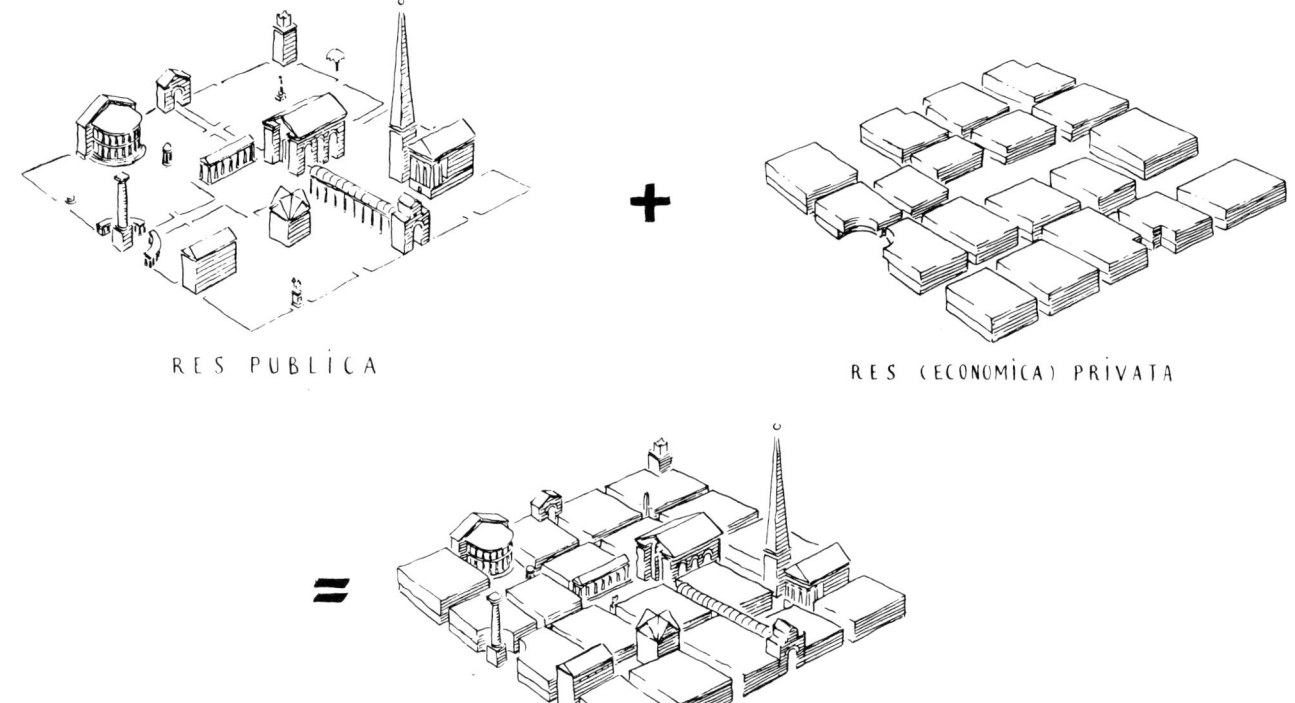

Domestic Building + Monumental Architecture = the CITY

A critique which has no project is but another face of a fragmented society, of which the city is the illustration.

A critique without a vision gazes as impotently at the future as the historian without a project gazes at the past.

Professional criticism has killed critique in the same way as historiography has killed history.

Our generation has to fight the destruction of urban society on all levels; cultural, political, economical.

Only with this project of reconstruction can we redefine our role as Architects, can we define what budgets this society has to allow to start this gigantic work of reconstruction.

It can no longer be short-term budgets that dictate the form of Architecture and of the City, rather Architecture and the City must dictate the form of long-term budgets.

This is the reason why we have to refuse to educate architects so that they know how to comply with the deficiencies of existing legislation and budgeting.

The Schools
An architectural culture must necessarily be based on a highly developed and professional manual culture.

The schools are the only places where the reconstruction of such a culture is possible, based on apprenticeship and temporarily freed from the contingencies of industrial production and the pressures of the building market.

Although schools and universities continue to live on the faded prestige and supremacy of intellectual over manual culture, intellectual work in advanced industrial societies has become as alienating and degrading as manual work.

These false myths could be definitely buried by giving a new social dignity to manual work, by conferring university diplomas to highly developed artisanal professions on the same level as scientific research, engineering, and the medical profession, all of which are ultimately based on manual work.

I do not believe that it is possible to re-educate modernist architects and planners, artists and teachers. Progress can only be made by founding elite institutions and educating a new generation of highly skilled and competitive artisans and architects. Their superior science and competence will soon achieve the restoration of dignity and secular authority to our prestigious art.

HERMAN HERTZBERGER
Apollo Schools, Amsterdam
1980-83

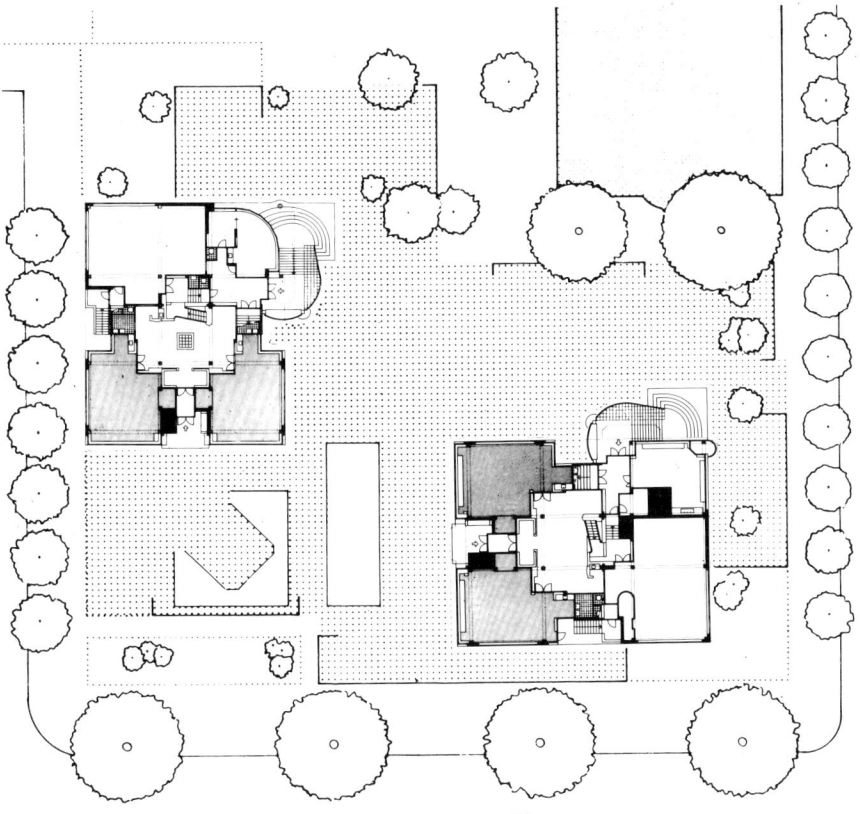

GROUND FLOOR PLANS

These two schools result from a double programme prescribed by the government, and because they were developed as twins from identical starting points, they consequently display many similarities.

The differences mainly result from their different positions on the site and the consequently different orientation of the bay windows of the classrooms, as well as the diverging of the two school councils which chose separate spatial organisations wherever the programme allowed.

Lastly, the future use of each school will eventually give its own colour. Space has been left for this freedom in all possible cases, especially where the dimensions were minimal.

The restricted building plot, situated beautifully in a large green area, inspired villa-like buildings which adapted themselves to the large detached houses lying adjacent to the townscape.

The interiors of both schools also comply with the image of a large villa; the classrooms are grouped around a hall, and open out onto the heart of the school, the central place for all activities which transcend the individual classrooms.

Both cube-like blocks are as closed to the outside as was demanded by the large outside space – a busy corner with heavy traffic noise – while on the inside everything is aimed at transparency, both spatially and organisationally.

Two Different Corner Solutions
Within the twin theme the question continuously arose if a similar or a different solution should be applied to each school and place.

One school is situated on the corner of the plot and the other further back. They have different positions in respect to the street. The outside spaces of both schools have therefore been formed differently and the entrances on the corners are approached differently.

In the Willems Park School this corner stands suspended in space, an effect strengthened by the receding curve. However, there was no reason for such a solution in the Montessori School which stands more or less at the edge of the plot with free space only on one side. This difference led to the different corner solutions next to the entrance staircases. The function of the rooms on the corners reinforced the motive: the Montessori School has a handiwork room on the corner with a small balcony, while the corner of the Willems Park School has the staff room with a clear view over the whole playground (one of their requirements).

Outside Stairways
The entrance balconies of the large stairways which allow admittance to the primary schools also form a shelter over the entrance to the infants' schools below.

The concrete stairs correspond to and unite with the concrete structure, thus forming a sort of core and the practical starting point of the building. A steel structure forms a lighter addition, its supple form and its greater transparency giving it a porch-like character which reduces an overall heaviness and prevents a negative, underworld-like effect underneath. By allowing the straight part of the stairs to begin at a landing already a number of steps above ground level, a space of restricted height was avoided underneath. This low landing with steps facing as many directions as possible offers the most self-evident approach from all directions as well as the opportunity to sit down with many different views.

Besides the steps, an informal opportunity to sit down is offered by the plinths in the way that they form the transition from the vertical surfaces to the ground.

Entrance Area to the Classrooms
The entrance areas to the classrooms have been strongly emphasised and have developed into complete study areas with a writing desk and a small bench surrounded by a low wall.

These places increase the openness of the classrooms towards the hall because one can work independently in the hallway – outside the classroom but not excluded . . .

To adjust the contact between the two in as many nuances as possible, 'half doors' have

The structural principle underlying this pair of schools may be summed up in the twenty intersection points shown below. Each of these solutions is derived from a common root, as it were the conjugation of a verb, and together they constitute a grammar: the construction as architectural order.

The drawings are shown in random sequence, and are classifiable according to varying interpretations, such as: interior and exterior; skeleton or consequential filling in with masonry, framing, steel fittings; cantilever, normal or extended; cross-beams or T-joists.

No attempt has been made to suppress certain salient features by simplification and, just as in language, exceptions to the grammatical rules have been made wherever necessary for the sake of expressing a particular point.

been used, their ambivalence providing for a feeling of both enclosure and openness simultaneously. Next to the door is a showcase for the display of work or exhibits, a small museum for each class.

Amphitheatre/Hall
The centre hall allows large or small groups to give performances. The space is not too small when occupied by the whole school at one time. The big steps which form the split level fulfil the task of an amphitheatre: as a result there is no need to drag chairs around. However, the hall is not too big when occupied by only a few people. Again it is the articulatory effect of the steps that produces the necessarily smaller space for the smaller activities. They can also be used as tables and give a certain amount of shelter, providing the necessary intimacy for the more individual activities. As a form these steps are indeterminate because they can be utilised in different ways. They offer a challenge to find new ways to use them in each new situation.

The classrooms have been fitted with kitchen units with permanent work tables that connect to make large drawings and seat large groups. In the Montessori School, where the classical arrangement is no longer complied with (in contrast to the Willems Park School where the rectangular part of the classrooms was required to be clear of obstacles), the units have been positioned in free space. The Montessori staff themselves determined the final position in a way that avoided traditional classroom arrangement: their originality achieved a diagonal spatial organisation which is a stimulus for a dynamic utilisation of the space.

Urbanism of the Details
A whole building and also a small part of that building can explain itself by showing how it is put together, how it works and what it is for.

We tried to make all elements clearly comprehensible, both individually and in relation to each other, and in doing so to make each part a whole within itself. In this way the details become as important as the overall conception of the building itself. Part and whole determine each other reciprocally and need the same attention. This is just as true for town planning where the details are crucial. In urbanism other criteria may apply, but the way of thinking does not differ, as is the case with *the urbanism of the details* when designing a fence, for example.

Column and Step
Each step at the school entrance becomes a place for the children to sit, especially when a column offers support and makes the space more inviting. Where this is realised, form yields. Here again the saying 'form makes itself, and that it is less a question of invention than of carefully listening to what people and things want to be' applies.

Windowsill
In a classroom windowsills, shelves and ledges all offer possible places to display the innumerable, often fragile and breakable things which children make; therefore the more spaces there are the better. These are the things that allow children to appropriate their environment and thus make it friendlier. That is why we make them at every obvious opportunity.

AERIAL VIEW (PHOTO H HERTZBERGR)

MONTESSORI SCHOOL ENTRANCE (PHOTO FRITZ DIJKHOF)

WILLEMS PARK SCHOOL (PHOTO H HERTZBERGER)

CENTRAL HALL (PHOTO RONALD ROOZEN)

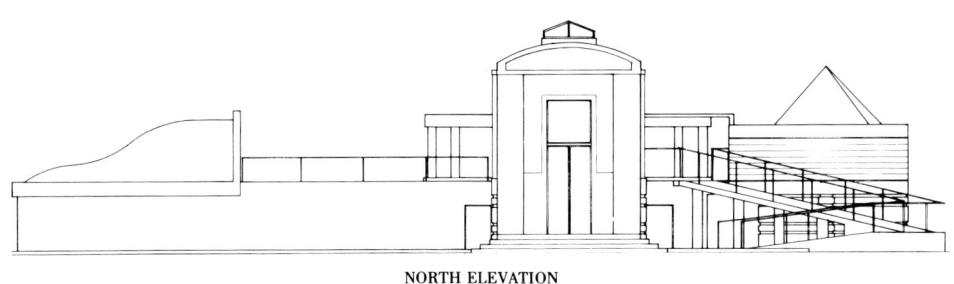
NORTH ELEVATION

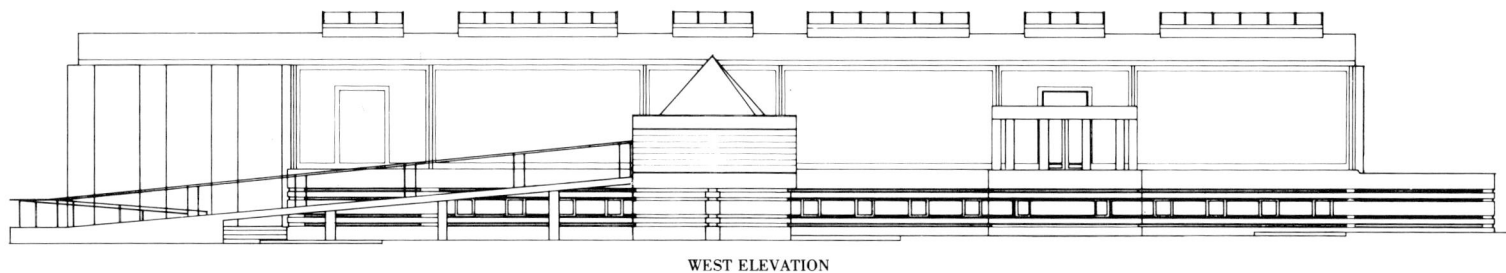
WEST ELEVATION

NORTH-SOUTH SECTION

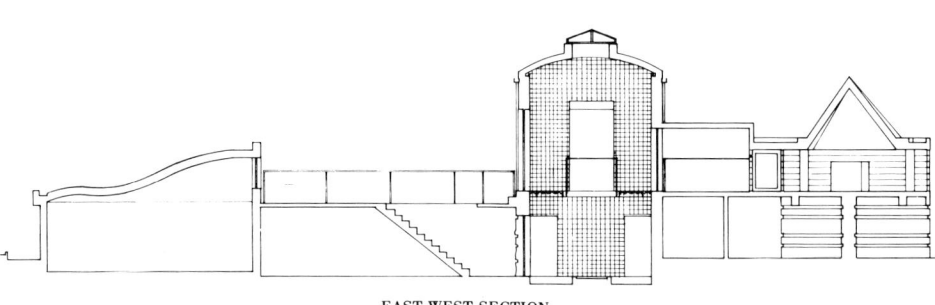
EAST-WEST SECTION

ARATA ISOZAKI
Okanoyama Graphic Art Museum
1982-84

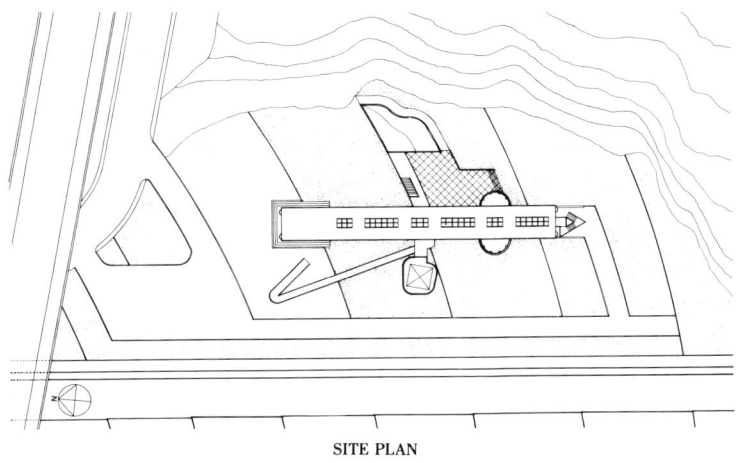

SITE PLAN

The Metaphor of the Train

This museum is in the suburbs of Nishiwaki, a small city of 40,000 to the northwest of Osaka. Nishiwaki is right in the geographical centre of the Japanese archipelago, and to mark its distinctive location the city has planned a park to be designed by Tadanori Yokoo. Yokoo, a native of the city, is a unique artist who has continued to produce since the 1960s some of the most innovative works of graphic art in Japan. For the project, which he has dubbed 'navel park,' Yokoo has proposed a ripple pattern spreading out from a centre and completely covering the surrounding landscape. However, it was decided to first build a museum to house records of Yokoo's career and his major works. A part of the proposed ripple pattern is used over the museum garden.

There are railway tracks by the site on which trains run a couple of times a day. A train metaphor was used, therefore, for the architectural image of this museum. Like a train with its concatenation of cars, the museum is composed of a series of connected galleries. The entrance is a portico with stout columns. The first room is devoted primarily to work from the sixties, the second to the seventies and the third to the eighties, all joined in chronological order. Yokoo, who was born in 1936, will no doubt continue to be active and develop different styles in future decades, necessitating the addition of many more units to the museum.

Since the interior spaces of the galleries needed to be as neutral as possible, the walls are simply painted white and lit by skylights. The vestibules linking these galleries have been specially designed to suggest in metaphorical fashion the theme with which the artist was preoccupied in each decade. For example, in the years around 1970 the idea of a southern paradise manifested itself in his works; one vestibule therefore will be brightly painted and have a palm tree planted in the middle. This vestibule leads to a cosmological, meditative space that suggests a pyramid of power.

A twisted, geometrical space is provided for the vestibule leading to the gallery devoted to Yokoo's work in the eighties when he became more and more radical and took a purely artistic approach. At the end of this series of galleries is an open stairway which will eventually be enclosed.

On the ground floor are an office, a seminar room and a storage room. Across a small courtyard is an atelier. These rooms will be used by art lovers in the district for their activities.

The ripple pattern of the park and the association with the train formed the outer context for the building. The inner context was the need to exhibit the radical development in the career of Tadanori Yokoo, an artist whose style has undergone a complete change approximately every ten years. From the disposition of the overall form to the treatment of the details, the building is meant to suggest metaphorical images that adapt it to these contexts. To provide a figurative (not abstract) exhibition space for the visitor to view the works and to do this within a small building of residential scale were the main objectives in designing this museum.

Arata Isozaki
Translated by HW

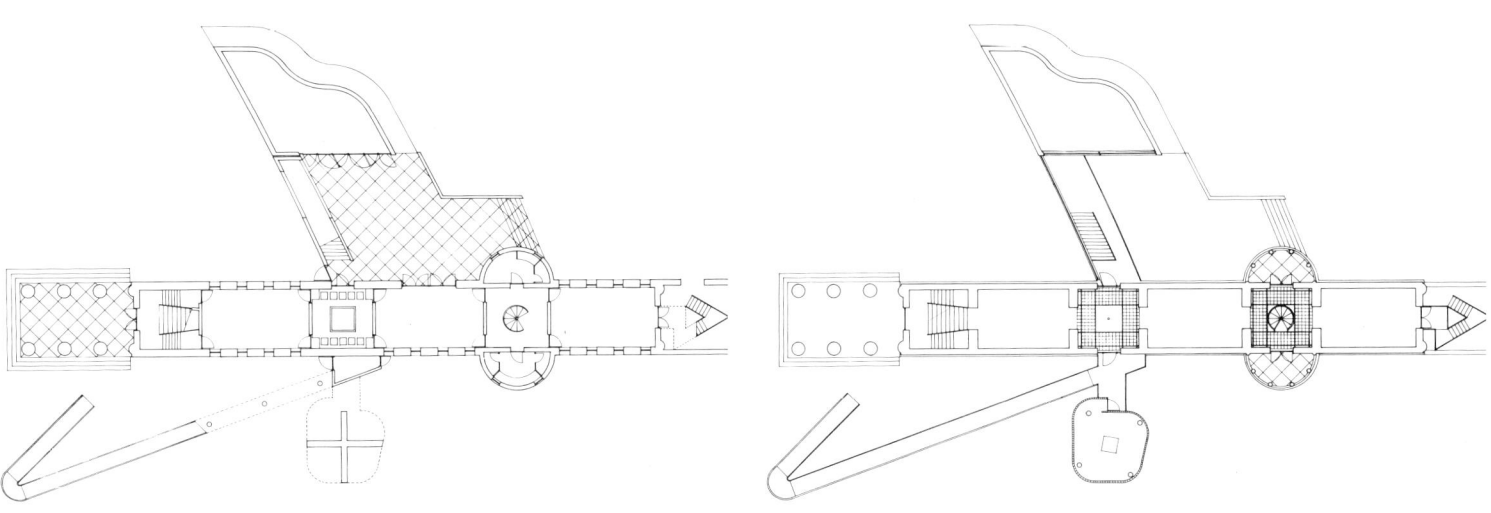

FIRST FLOOR PLAN
SECOND FLOOR PLAN

VIEW FROM WEST

VIEW TOWARD MEDITATION ROOM

MEDITATION ROOM

PORTICO

ENTRANCE HALL (CIRCULATION ROOM 1)

1960s GALLERY

CIRCULATION ROOM 3 (ALL PHOTOS Y FUTUGAWA)

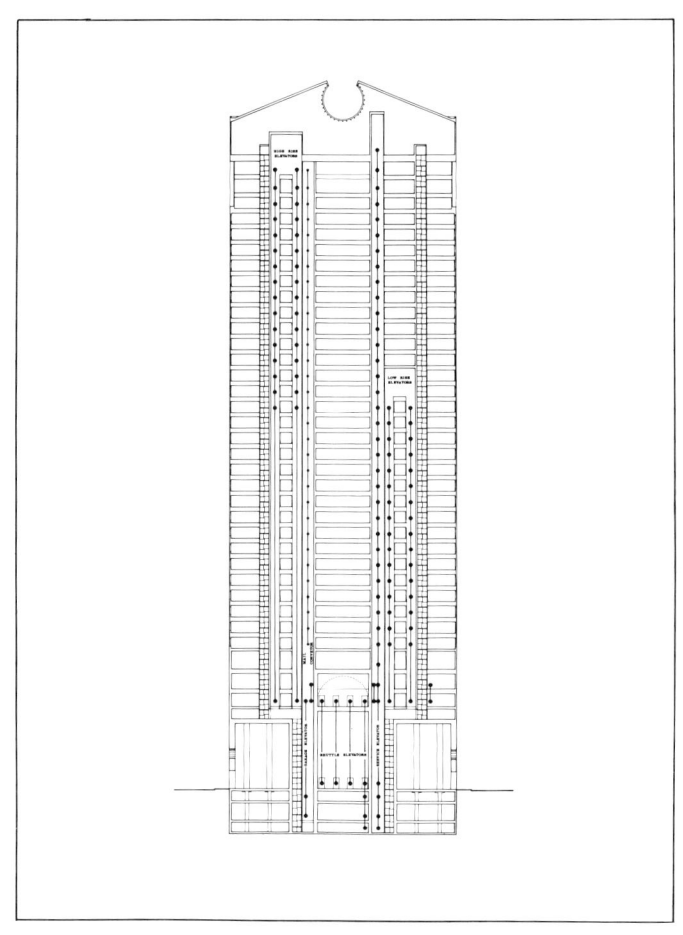

SECTION SHOWING VERTICAL CIRCULATION

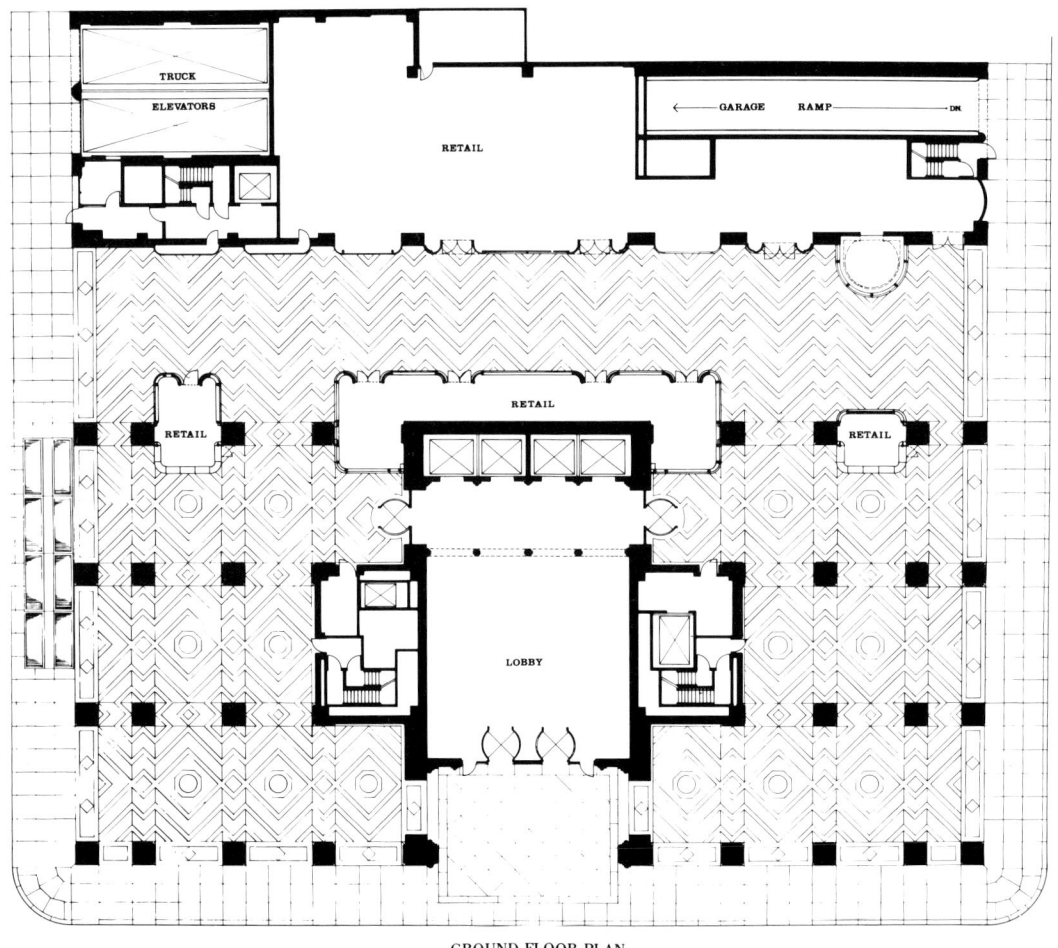

GROUND FLOOR PLAN

PHILIP JOHNSON
&
JOHN BURGEE
AT&T Corporate Headquarters, NYC
1978-83

VIEW FROM 56TH STREET (PHOTO C JENCKS)

The 195 Broadway Corporation has built the corporate headquarters of the American Telephone and Telegraph Company on a 36,800 ft^2 site on the west side of Madison Avenue between East 55th and East 56th Streets.

The building complex consists of a 37-floor office tower raised 60 feet above street level on an open colonnade, a three-storey annexe structure, a glass-covered pedestrian gallery between the tower and the annexe, a pedestrian arcade on the street beneath the raised office tower, and three underground levels.

The 648 ft tower, which has a sloped-roof apex, is serviced by shuttle elevators transporting people from a street-level lobby to a sky lobby which contains the general building elevator banks, lounges and dining conference facilities. Above it, an open level accommodates employee dining rooms. Each of the 37 floors in the tower has a gross floor area of approximately 19,300 ft^2; the entire complex has a total gross floor area of 850,300 ft^2. Two of the 37 floors house mechanical equipment, another two house the sky lobby facilities, and one is taken up by an elevator pit. The remaining 32 floors are for office facilities.

The annexe structure on the western side of the tower contains shops at the street level. They face the glass-covered pedestrian space between the annexe and the tower arcade. Also on the ground level is the entrance to the multi-media exhibit centre and the science museum on the upper two levels of the annexe. Other facilities in the annexe include a ramp for a 50-space underground car park opening onto East 56th Street, two truck lifts for service entry to the off-street loading dock facilities opening onto East 55th Street, and the emergency generating system for the entire complex.

The 'Galleria', a pedestrian space modelled after the Galleria in Milan, is covered by a 100 ft transparent roof which connects the annexe to the 'Loggia', an arcade under the raised tower.

The arcade, which is 60 ft high, is defined on the north and south by light-penetrating skirting (to brace the columns on which the tower stands) and textured by highly articulated columns and ceiling designs.

The pedestrian space and the arcade are open to the public, subject to reasonable rules and regulations. The open areas allow free and random pedestrian movement throughout the site to the surrounding shops and buildings. Covering more than 37,000 ft^2, these areas enrich the special shopping character of the Madison Avenue district. Here, tables and chairs offer a protected and restful place in the city and kiosk vendors sell special food and drinks. Bordering on the Galleria are also small boutiques which interlock with the rear tower colonnade and the exhibit centre and museum by means of a glass-encased vertical exterior elevator. The building complex will attract thousands of visitors who will use the commercial facilities in the area. The public pedestrian spaces also relate to the public spaces in the IBM building across East 56th Street.

The floor areas used to encourage greater public activity in and around the site are as follows: a) the arcade (Loggia) under the tower including columns – 14,380 ft^2; b) the covered pedestrian space (Galleria) – 5,852 ft^2; c) the commercial shops and the kiosks for the food vendors – 4,700 ft^2; d) the annexe used for the multi-media exhibit centre and the science museum – 12,672 ft^2.

Three levels beneath the entire complex contain parking facilities, off-street loading docks, mechanical and maintenance equipment and storage.

Collaborators: Harry Simmons-Brooklyn (Associate Architect); HRH Construction Co (Construction Manager).

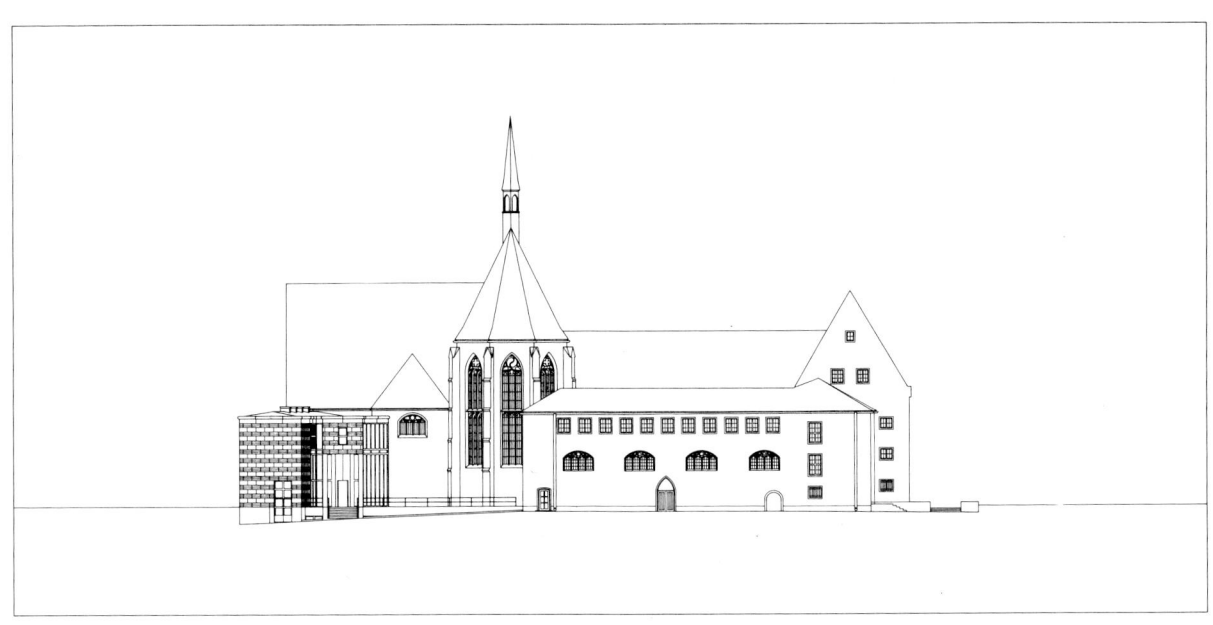
EAST ELEVATION

NORTH ELEVATION WITH SECTION THROUGH TRANSEPT

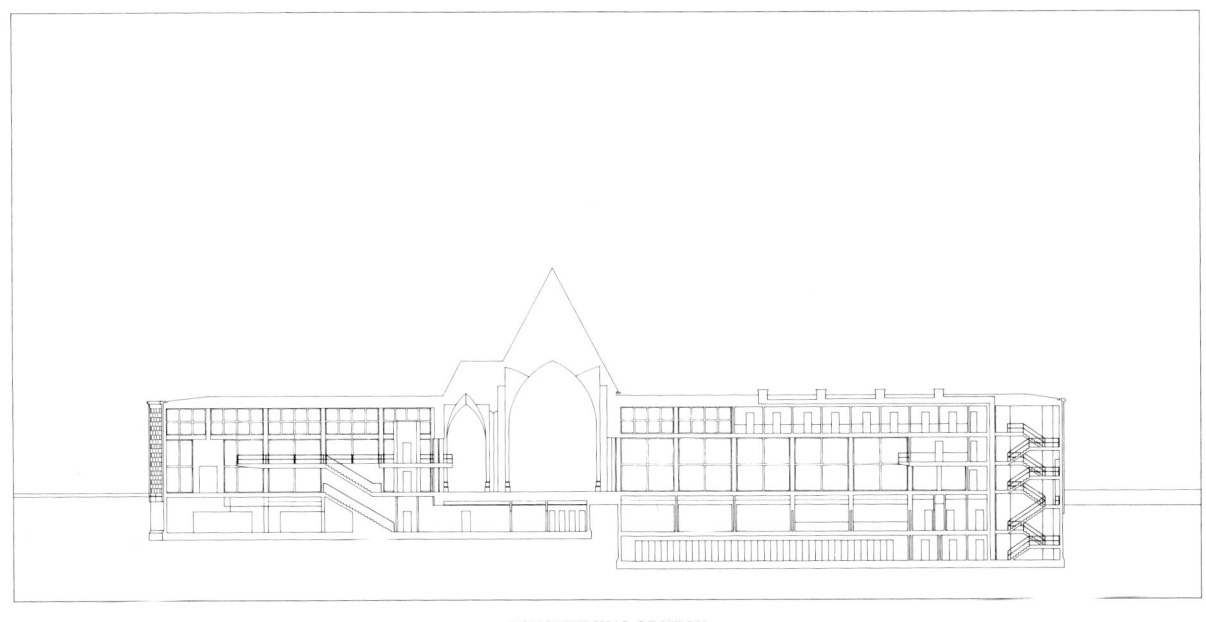
LONGITUDINAL SECTION

JOSEF PAUL KLEIHUES
Museum of Pre- and Early History at Frankfurt 1980-84

SOUTH ELEVATION

The traditional role of museums has been to collect, catalogue, preserve, display and educate. More recently, they have also become places of relaxation and contemplation, though this fact has been overlooked in some of the newer museum buildings. In the Frankfurt Museum of Prehistory and Early History, however, the museum's function as a source of intellectual and sensuous pleasure for the visitor is given equal ranking with the traditional roles.

A museum can have an efficient functional layout and a pleasing environment. One does not preclude the other. Thus the exhibition spaces are arranged *spatially and architectonically*, and the storage, restoration and administrative areas are arranged *spatially and functionally*, as follows.

Organisational Concept
The exhibition spaces are exclusively on the main level (which comprises the entry and the church). The storerooms, archives and restoration workshops are concentrated on the first level of the basement, with additional storage in a second level below. The administrative and educational areas are on the upper level.

The exhibition spaces are tied to the restoration and storage areas by a hydraulic service lift. A stairway and a passenger lift at the separate administrative entrance on Karmelitergasse provide additional links between all the different levels.

Urban Planning/Architectonic Concept
The most decisive factor in the urban planning concept was the Carmelite monastery in general, and its chapel in particular. Firstly, nothing large could be built over the existing buildings, so the storerooms and restoration workshops were placed below, in a two-level basement. Secondly, the architectonic emphasis of the restoration had to be decided. Our proposal had the following characteristics: emphasis of the morphological layering from north to south (with marked longitudinal tendencies from east to west) through parallel construction to the Alte Mainzer Gasse; emphasis of the opening of the block concept to Karmeliter and Seckbacher Streets and the resulting 'elevation' of the church choir; and emphasis of the wings of the Carmelite church through enclosure on both sides by the Alte Mainzer Gasse.

The concept aims at the introversion of the complex as a whole, so the exhibit areas look to the north with views of the Carmelite monastery and church and at the same time turn towards the simple green courtyards between the new museum structure and the monastery. The emphasised openings to the north make reference to the play between shadow and light in the old building and largely dispense with the need for protection from the sun. In contrast, the openings on the wall opposite the Alte Mainzer Gasse are purely functional, emphasising the closed nature of the complex.

Construction and Materials
The closed walls on the street side are of lightweight concrete with 0.45m wide pilasters spaced at 5.40m intervals. They are covered with red/brown and grey/green natural stone panels in two different sizes (0.45m x 0.90m and 0.45 x 0.45m). The composition of the wall is 0.20m lightweight concrete, 0.05m insulation, 0.05m air space and 0.10m stone veneer, making a total width of 0.45m.

The exhibition and administrative areas opening onto the side of the courtyard are triple glazed. The columns, which are 0.45m by 0.45m, are either entirely of reinforced concrete, or of concrete with natural stone cladding.

The window constructions consist of 'separated steel profiles' which are screwed together over the core of insulation.

Colouring
Colours were chosen to match the colours used in the Carmelite monastery and Frankfurt's old quarter when they were originally built. The pilasters, socles and mouldings are of red 'Main' sandstone, and the alternating panels on the walls are of red 'Main' sandstone and grey/green shell limestone.

Collaborators: Mirko Baum, Thomas Bartels, Siobhán Ni Éanaigh, Günter Sunderhaus.

Translated by Pamela Johnston

AXONOMETRIC

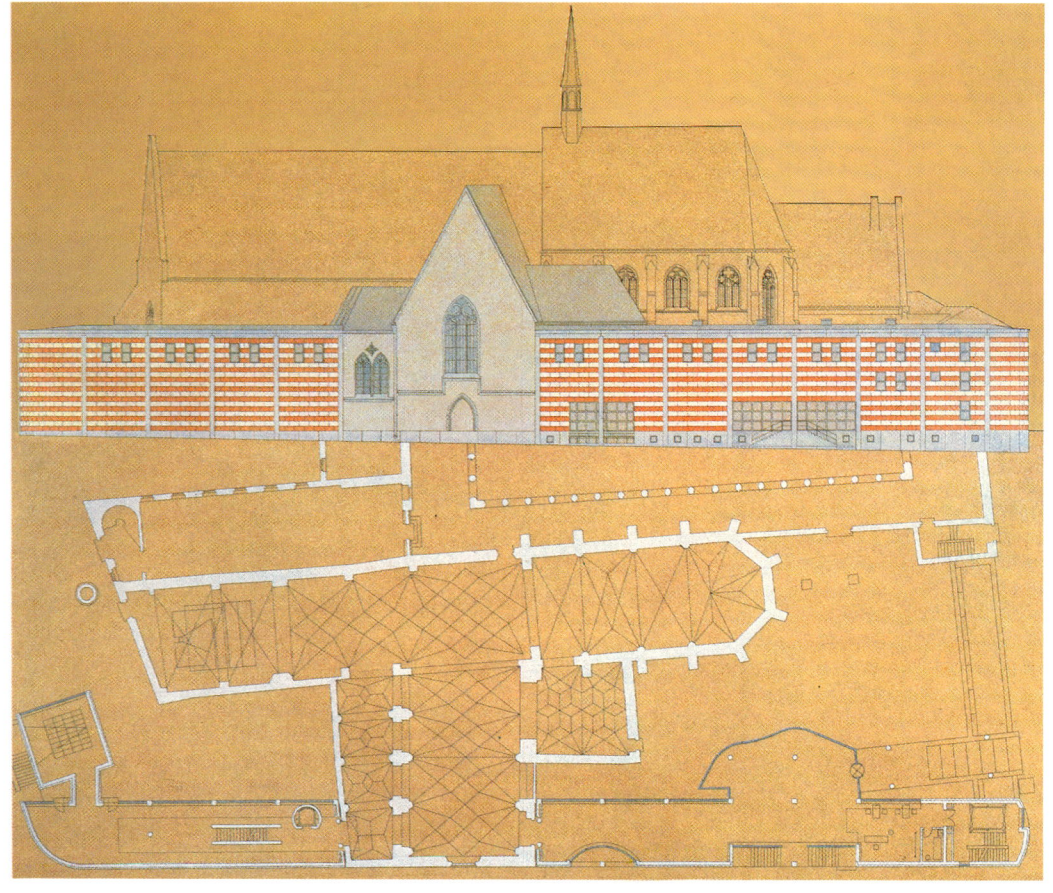

SOUTH ELEVATION AND PLAN

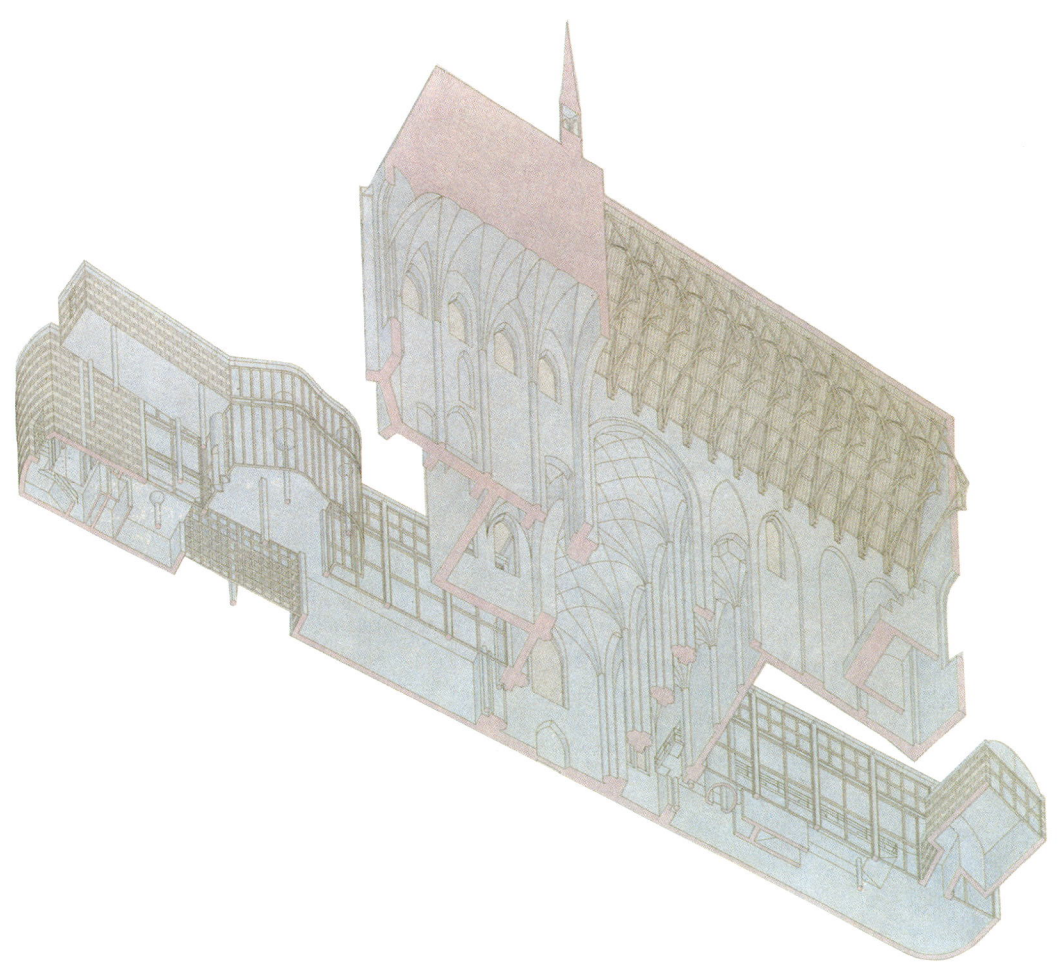

CUT-AWAY UP AXONOMETRIC

NORTH ELEVATION

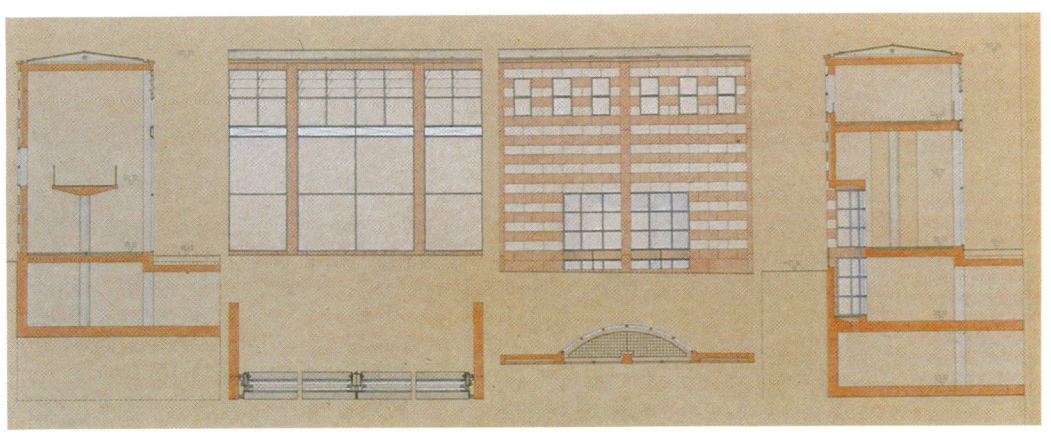

FACADE DETAILS

RICHARD MEIER & PARTNERS
The High Museum of Art, Atlanta, Georgia 1980-83

ENTRANCE FROM PEACHTREE STREET

Most of the great European museums are conversions from grand residences or palaces, and the older objects in their collections are seen in natural light in the large-scale environment for which they were created. Today, however, the scale of the objects and our expectations have changed, and natural light is often considered harmful. The High Museum of Art attempts to resolve the best of old and modern notions of the art museum. On one hand, it refers to the typological tradition of the Enlightenment, when museums came to have an educational as well as collecting role; on the other, it attempts to encourage discovery of aesthetic values and convey a sense of the museum as a contemplative place. The circulation, lighting, installation and spatial qualities of the design are intended to encourage people to experience the art of architecture as well as the art displayed.

The design of the museum developed as a series of architectonic responses to context in the broadest sense, which was understood to include not only functional, pragmatic and typological concerns, but also the physical, social and historical context of the city. The museum is located at the corner of Peachtree and Sixteenth Streets, about two miles from downtown Atlanta. The site is an important one for the future development of the city, being adjacent to the Memorial Arts Center and the First Presbyterian Church, and within a pedestrian-oriented neighbourhood accessible by good public transport. The *parti* consists of four quadrants, with one carved out to create a monumental quarter-circle atrium. To preserve the beautiful tree-lined frontage on Peachtree, the atrium is located next to the Memorial Arts Center and set well back from the street: entry is by way of a long ramp which projects out of the building on the diagonal of the site, taking the visitor along a screen wall, through a portico, and into the main level of the museum. The extended exterior ramp is both a symbolic gesture reaching out to the city and a foil to the tensile quarter-circle interior ramp, which is the building's chief formal and circulatory element. In plunging into the heart of the building, the diagonal of the entry ramp disrupts the classical four-square symmetry of the plan and initiates a set of more turbulent geometries which successively inflect the architectural order.

On the left of the entry ramp is the main museum building. Next to it, at a 45° angle, is the cubic volume of a 200-seat auditorium. The auditorium is treated as separate from the main building for reasons of access and security, but its location reinforces the processional sequence: entry is by the end of the ramp through a neck between a convex wall and the volume itself, and exit is by way of a second ramp running in reverse beside the first one, producing a continuous loop of movement in and out of the auditorium.

At the right end of the ramp is a piano-curved element. This is the main entry/reception area leading into the four-storey skylit atrium. To some extent this dramatic central space is inspired by (and comments on) the Guggenheim Museum. A curved ramp and gallery spaces encircle the atrium, which becomes the fixed point of reference for movement up and around the galleries. As in the Guggenheim, the ramp system mediates between the light-filled central space and the art itself, which may be viewed and reviewed from various levels, angles and distances as one moves upward. The problem with the Guggenheim is that the ramp is made to double as a gallery, inducing movement rather than contemplative viewing. The sloping floor plane, ceilings and walls are not only uncomfortable but also impractical because they suppress the datum of the right angle, making the display of paintings especially difficult. In Atlanta, the separation of circulation and gallery space overcomes these problems and also allows the atrium walls to have windows which admit natural light and offer framed views of the city. The galleries can receive either natural or artificial light depending on the requirements of the art displayed, and are organised to provide intimate and larger-scale viewing to accommodate the diverse needs of the collection, as well as multiple vistas, cross-references and glimpses across the atrium from one exhibition space to another. Here the spatial variety and clearly apparent relationship of the plan parts

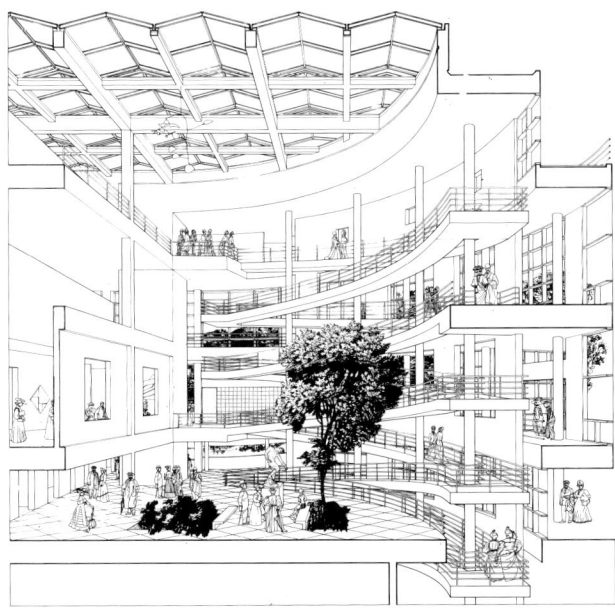

PERSPECTIVE OF ATRIUM

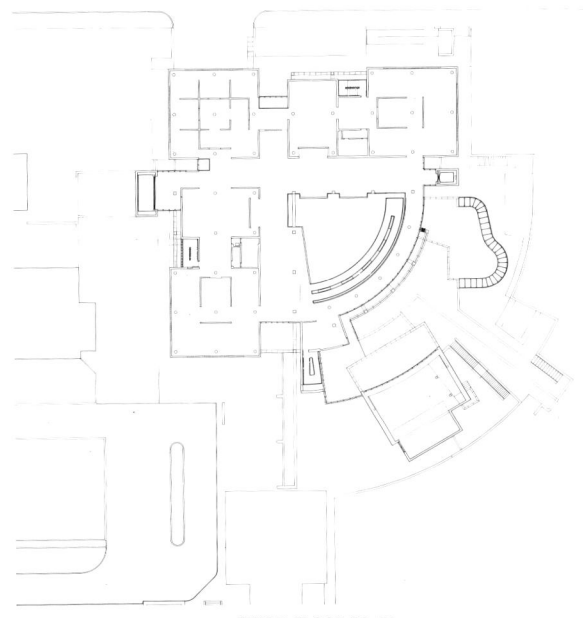

THIRD FLOOR PLAN

afforded by the atrium help alleviate the experience of fatigue to which one often succumbs in large museums.

Within the 130,000 ft² building are 52,000 ft² of gallery space. Off the ground floor court are a café with kitchen, museum shop and members' lounge, and – behind a wall used for exhibiting new acquisitions – the director's and curators' offices, staff spaces and boardroom. The counter-clockwise ramp to the upper floor galleries takes one roughly chronologically through the history of art; stairs and an elevator provide alternative means of circulation. The top floor is shared by twentieth-century art and loan exhibitions; the loan space can expand into the twentieth-century space as necessary to accommodate major shows. The auditorium, which is separate from the main building at entry level, may be entered from within at a second level balcony: this allows it to function as an integral part of the museum when desired. The educational spaces – junior galleries, workshops, department offices – are situated on the floor below the main level. They have their own entrance off Sixteenth Street, so that children coming by bus can go directly into the building under cover. Storage areas and other service and mechanical spaces are also located on this level.

The structure consists of steel columns and frame and concrete slabs. The granite base acts as a horizontal datum for the ramps and an anchor for the white porcelain-enamelled panels cladding the galleries above.

Light is a constant preoccupation throughout, whether it is direct or filtered, or admitted through skylights, ribbon glazing, clerestory strips or minimal perforations in the panel wall. Apart from its functional role, it also has a symbolic role showing the museum as a place of aesthetic illumination and enlightened cultural values. The total architecture is intended to encourage the discovery of these values and foster a contemplative appreciation of the museum's collection through its own spatial experience.

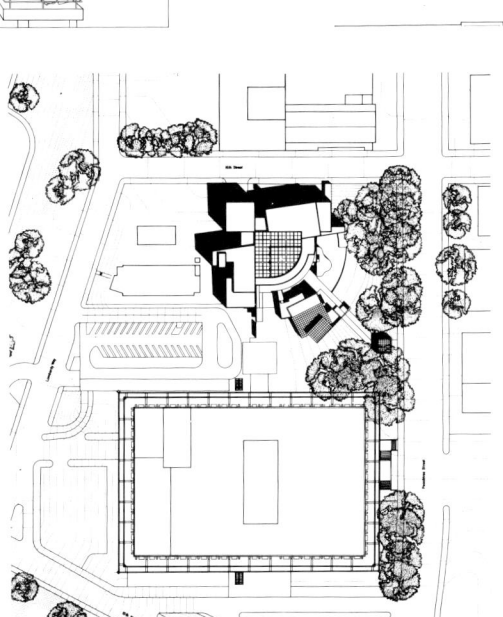

SITE PLAN

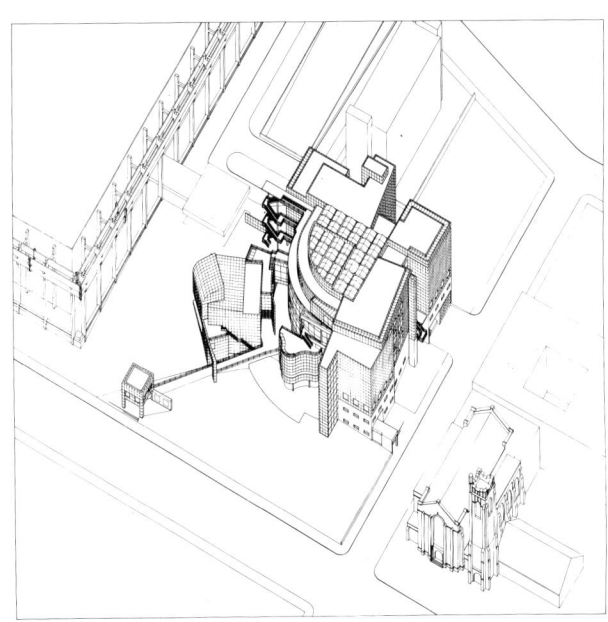

AXONOMETRIC VIEW FROM NORTHEAST

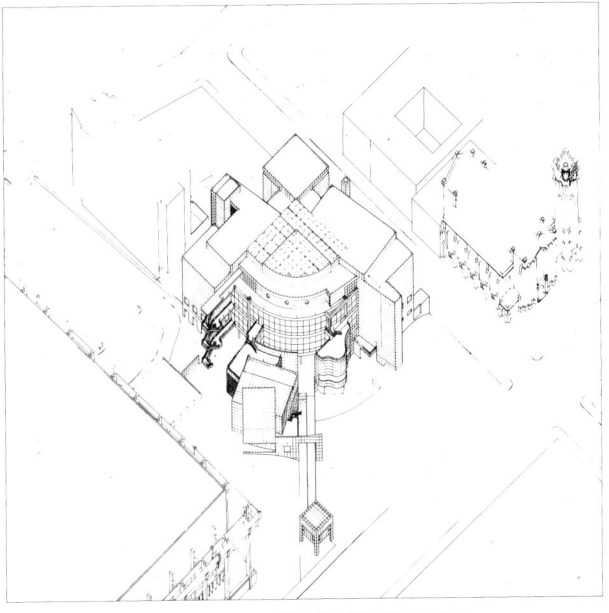

AXONOMETRIC VIEW FROM SOUTHEAST

VIEW FROM THE NORTHEAST

VIEW FROM THE RAMP

VIEWS OF THE ATRIUM (ALL PHOTOS EZRA STOLLER © ESTO PHOTOGRAPHICS INC)

VIEW FROM THE RUE JEAN NICOT

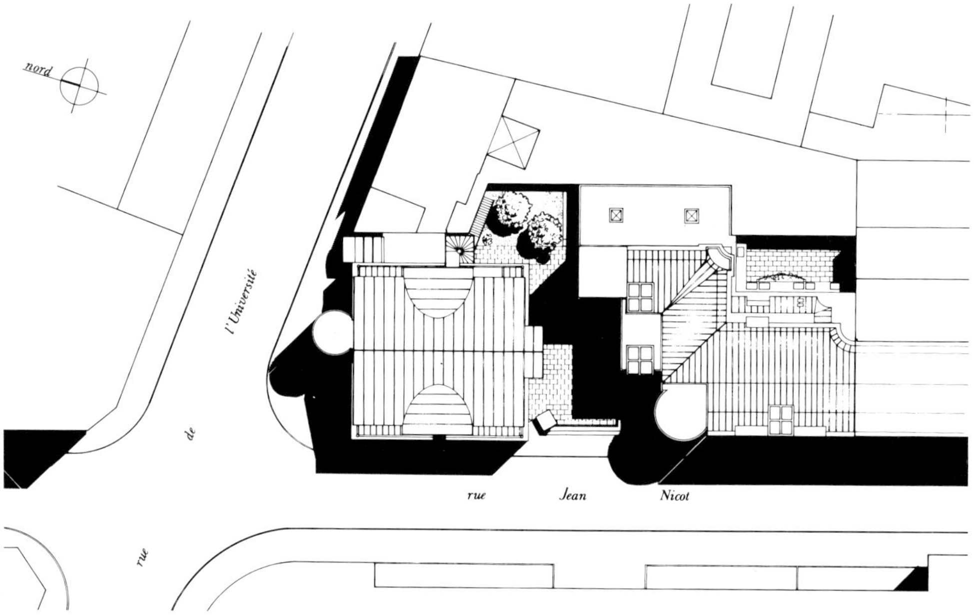

SITE PLAN

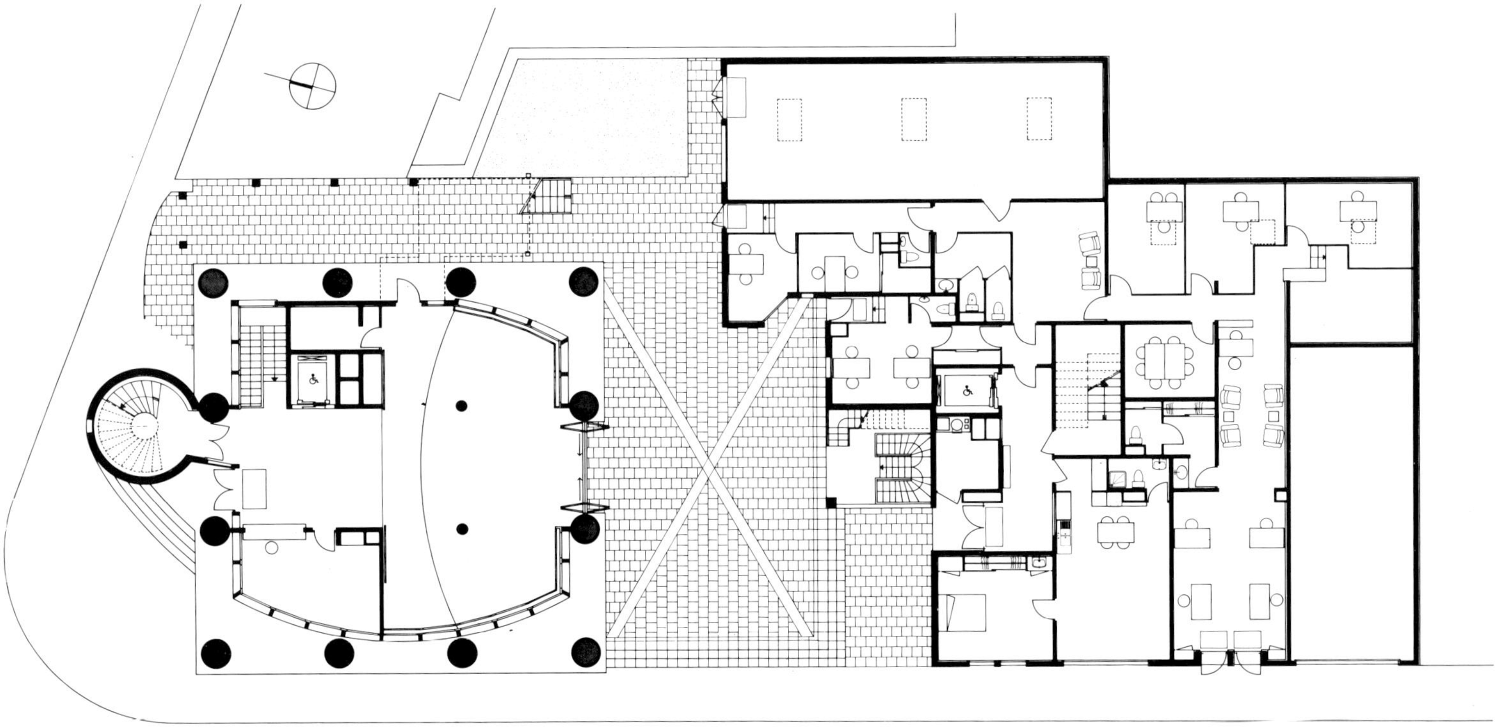

GROUND FLOOR PLAN

CHRISTIAN DE PORTZAMPARC
Conservatory of Music and Retirement Home, Paris 1981-84

VIEW FROM THE RUE DE L'UNIVERSITE

Urban Integration
The building that Christian de Portzamparc has just completed in the seventh arrondissement of Paris is remarkable in more than one respect. Rather than being just one building, it is in fact two. On one side, dramatically situated at the corner of the Rue de l'Université, is the Paris Conservatory of Music, Dance and Dramatic Art, a sort of isolated 'temple' which immediately projects the idea of a public building; on the other side is the retirement home which is aligned more simply with the continuous facades of the homes on Rue Jean Nicot.

In between the Conservatory and the retirement home a small square has been created which puts the two buildings in tension and at the same time reveals – contrary to normal city typology – the 'tower' of a neighbouring building situated in the heart of the block. The design thus results from a work of fragmentation: the distinction made between the programmes for the home and the Conservatory ensures the relative autonomy of each building and at the same time offers the city an additional public space. Moreover, this fragmentation means that fragments on the outer limits of the project itself can be brought into the architectural composition. [The architect thus] changes the way in which the problem of urban integration is usually presented. He does not always mimetically follow the lay-out of the streets but rather attempts to reveal and to integrate the elements of the immediate environment in order to create an architectural method and produce a series of urban relations in an interplay of multiple polarities.

Unity and Fragmentation
This fragmentation is an architectural and urban study which Christian de Portzamparc has been pursuing for several years now. In this light, one must take a new look at his work: the group of 'Hautes Formes' (High Forms) which he built in the thirteenth arrondissement in 1975, the housing projects which he exhibited at La Saltpétrière in 1981, Evry, Enghein, Marne la Vallée, or his recent projects which were exhibited at the French Institute of Architecture this summer. The Conservatory and the retirement home represent one more step in the development of an architectural language of great coherence. [The architect] sees the city of today as multipolar, composed of confrontations and superimpositions, a heterogeneous space that is sometimes animated, other times anguishing, often empty of sense; he sees it as a world that we are forced to confront. Nonetheless, he has never resorted to 'collage' to form his architecture.

In the case of the Conservatory, two principle characteristics may be observed: first, the archetypal figures, which may be fairly easily analysed in the case of the temple-like Conservatory with its thick stone pillars, smooth surfaces and pediments crowning the top of the building; secondly, the relations of the assembled, half-put-together fragments of architecture. This last notion is certainly the more mysterious one because it demands to be read with close attention but without any attachment to the dialectic that may sometimes seem, at first sight, to be a formal *a priori* choice. This exploration does not extend to researching a pure object with indivisible surfaces. For all that, it is never guided by arbitrary factors. Far from it. It attempts to discover an architectural 'syntax'.

The architecture of the Conservatory may thus be read as an architecture which explores an unknown dimension of architectural language without resorting to obvious quotations, trying instead to recall multiple evocations of past architectures.
Jacques Lucan

See also AD 51 12-1981, pp 130-3

EXTERIOR AND INTERIOR VIEWS OF THE CONSERVATORY OF MUSIC

SITE PLAN

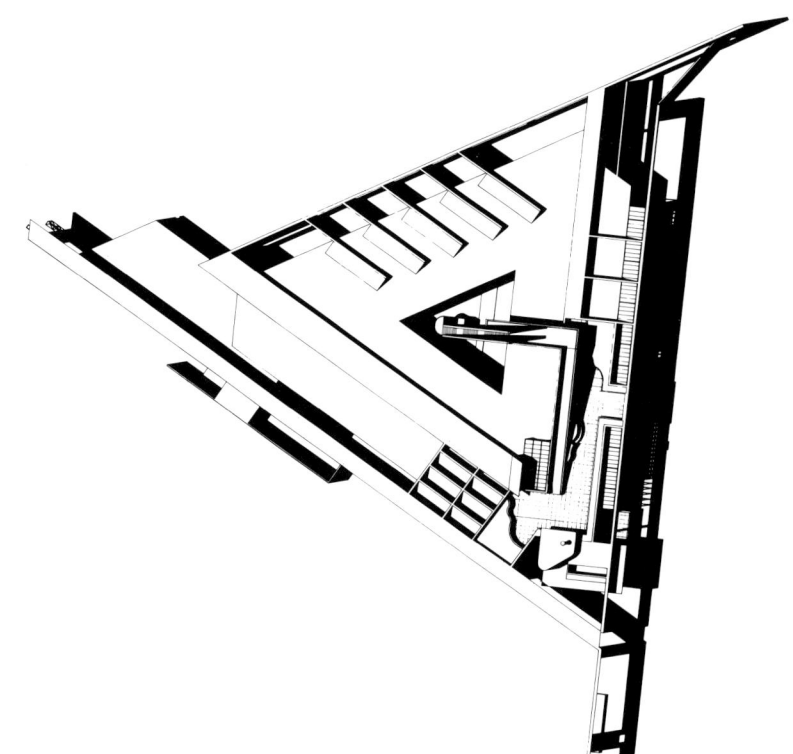

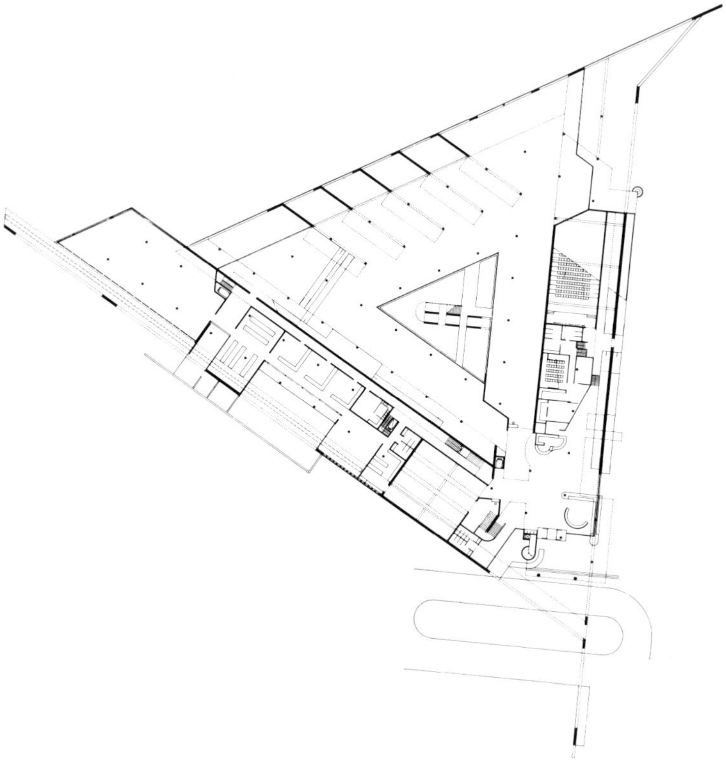

GROUND FLOOR PLAN

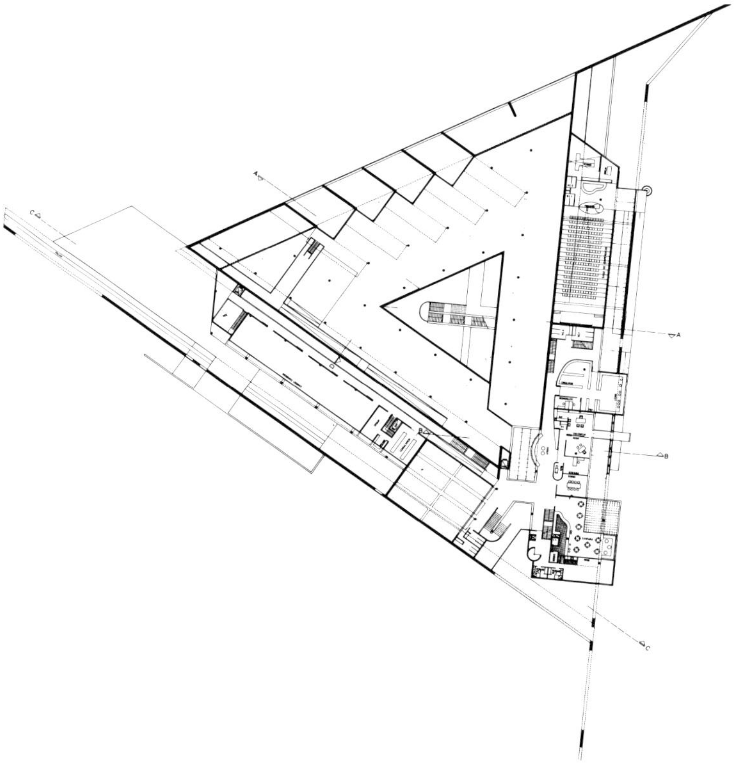

UPPER LEVEL PLAN

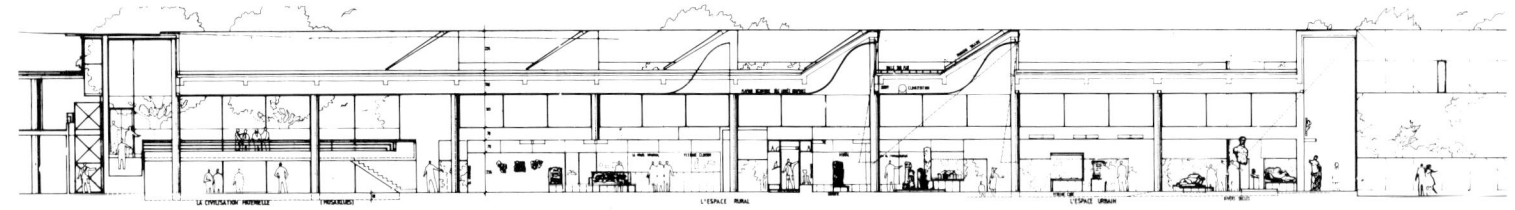

TYPICAL SECTION

HENRI CIRIANI
Archaeological Museum at Arles 1984

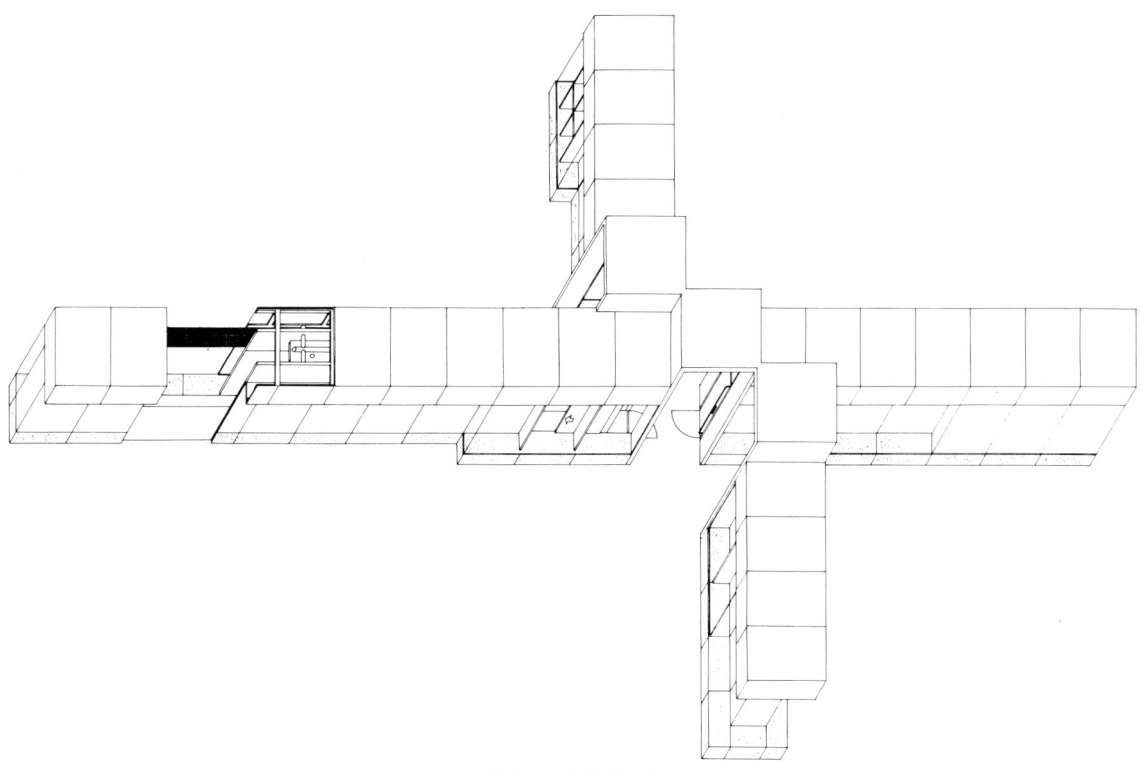

PERMANENT DISPLAY

This project was the winning entry in a two-stage competition to design a museum of archaeology for Arles. The site is located south-east of the historic centre of the town on a peninsula in the river Rhône containing a Roman arena.

The brief calls for approximately 6,000 square metres of building, to be broken down as follows: lobby 400m²; permanent display 2,800 m²; temporary display 300 m²; meeting rooms, library, educational services, restaurant 840 m²; ancillary 700 m²; store 900 m²; administration, personnel 200 m²; technical equipment 200 m². The budget is 48 million francs.

Context
Before the peninsula can act as mediator between the ancient and the new town the whole site must be given a single conceptual order, that of a 'campo santo' (sacred compound). The new museum will occupy a position secondary to that of the old Roman arena which runs the whole length of the site in liaison with the ancient town. The building will therefore have to have a strong form, pure and recognisable.

The lock will be integrated with the urban composition through a dialogue with the museum (the triangle) and the palace of congress (the square). Facing the viaduct which overhangs the site, the museum will present itself as the 'backdrop' for the arena. In widening out towards the point of the peninsula, it forms a triangle.

Function
Because of the nature of the objects on display, the exhibition spaces will have to be on a single level. Visitors will have a choice between two circuits: one is long and the other short, but they both converge on the same point, the hall, which is the core of the museum. Attached to this space are two wings: the one on the south will eventually house the library, which will back up to partition walls allowing room for expansion of the permanent exhibition. The other wing will contain spaces arranged to mirror the old Roman arena facing it: one thus moves from the first access portico to the cloister-portico in the mosaic courtyard, across the hall to the grand staircase with its belvedere to the cafe terrace and the temporary exhibition.

The orientation of the site dictated the choice of fenestration: a complete opacity will face the sun on the lock side and window shuttering with a vertical protection will counter the Mistral on the river side.

Form and Matter
An open form will be created with a closed plan.

The dynamics of the triangle will be preserved by assuring the autonomy of the three double partitions that delineate it.

The triangle is the best form for the path around the museum because it provides a direct route to follow but still leaves room for deeper exploration.

The triangle puts the museum and the arena in a situation of tension in relation to the peninsula. The vast space within the museum is made emotive by the quality of light in it (the building looks north). The floor is of grey stone and the precise interlacing structure is of matt white concrete. Different colours and materials will be brought in by the furniture, exhibit partitions and objects on display.

On the exterior, the horizontal surfaces will be treated in terracotta and the vertical ones in blue Emalit (the colour of the sky above Arles), as a sign of the permanent place that the ancient town holds in the spirits of the people living there today and tomorrow.

Collaborators: Jacques Bajolle (Partner-in-Charge of Sitework); Michel Dayot, Jacques Garcin, Jacky Nicolas (Assistants); SCOBAT (Consultants); Patrick Berger (Model).

NORTHEAST ELEVATION

NORTHWEST ELEVATION

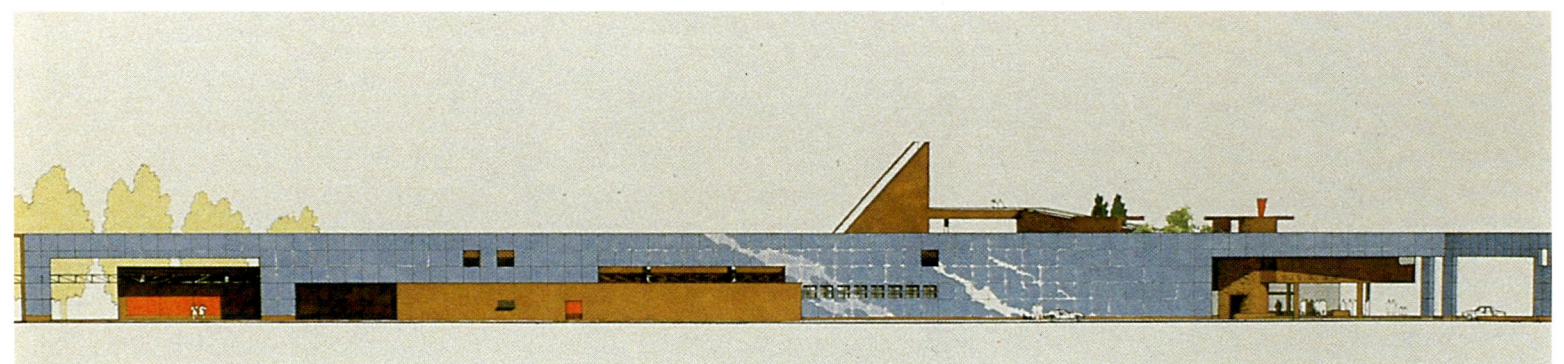
SOUTH ELEVATION

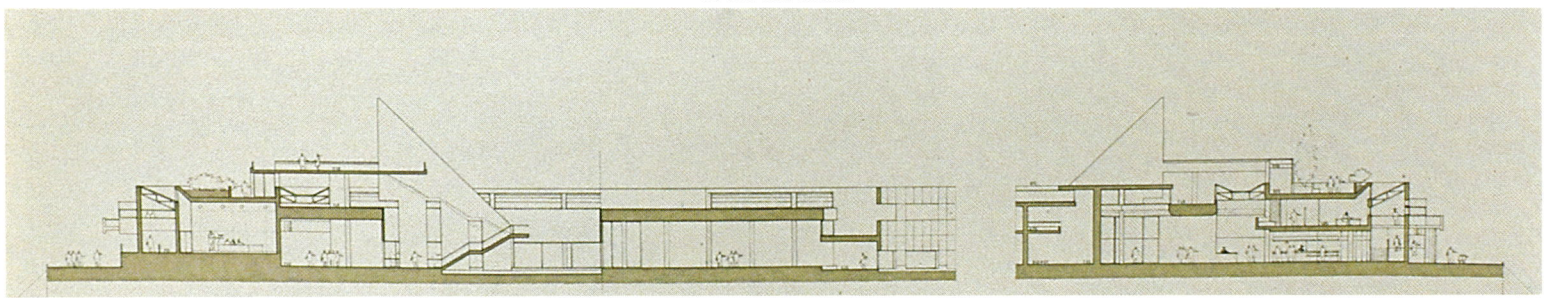
SECTION A-A   SECTION B-B

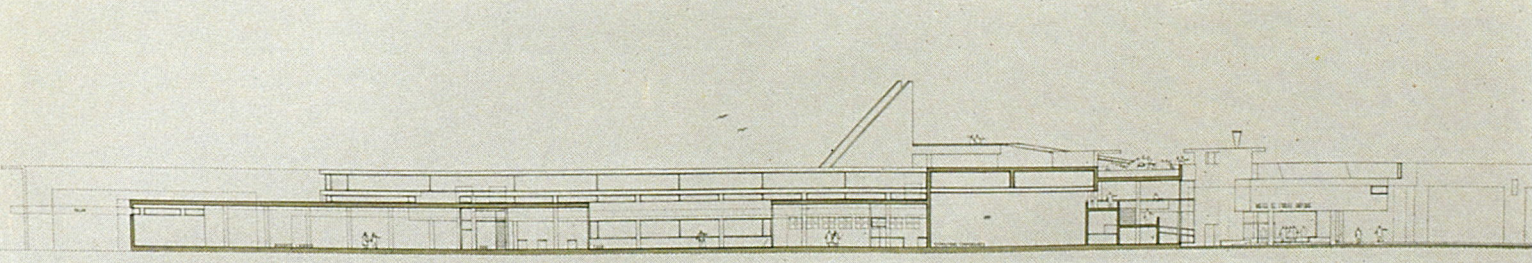
SECTION C-C   SCALE 1:200

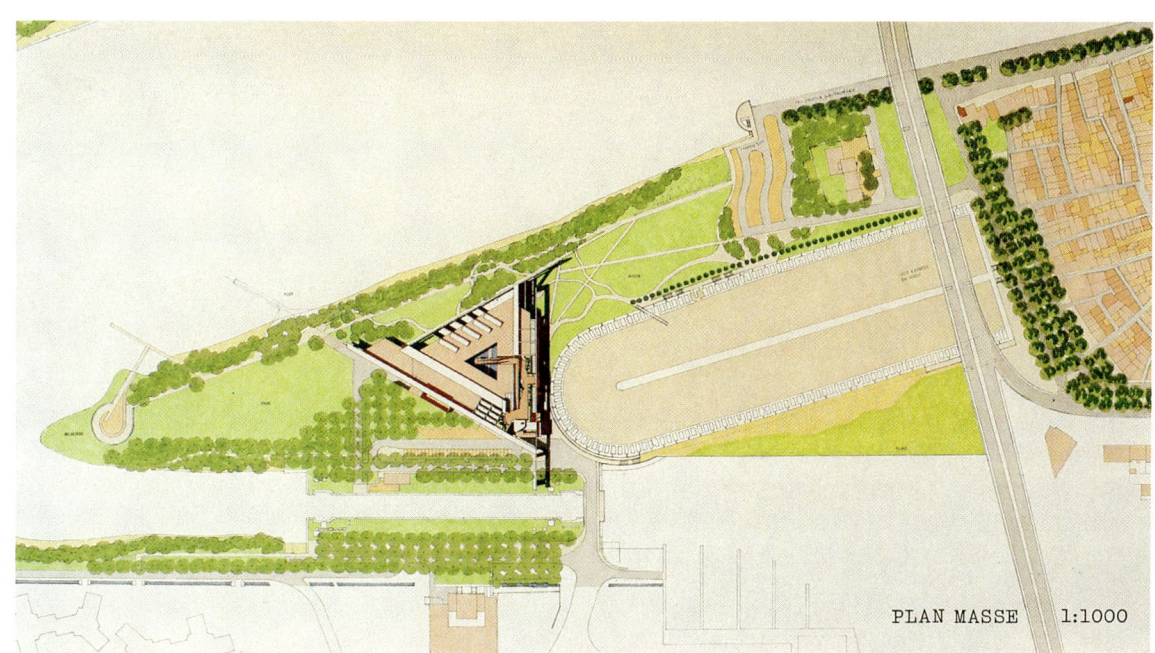
SITE PLAN

ENTRANCE SPACE

GALLERY OF SARCOPHAGI

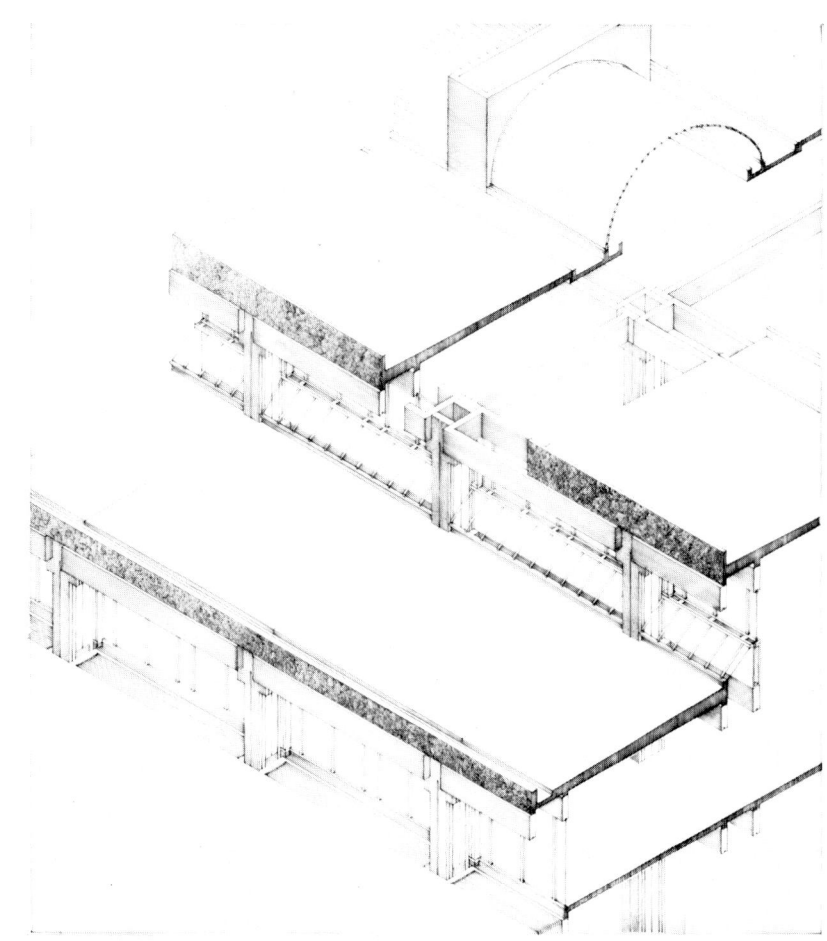

AXONOMETRIC SECTIONS OF THE DEPARTMENT OF CHEMISTRY

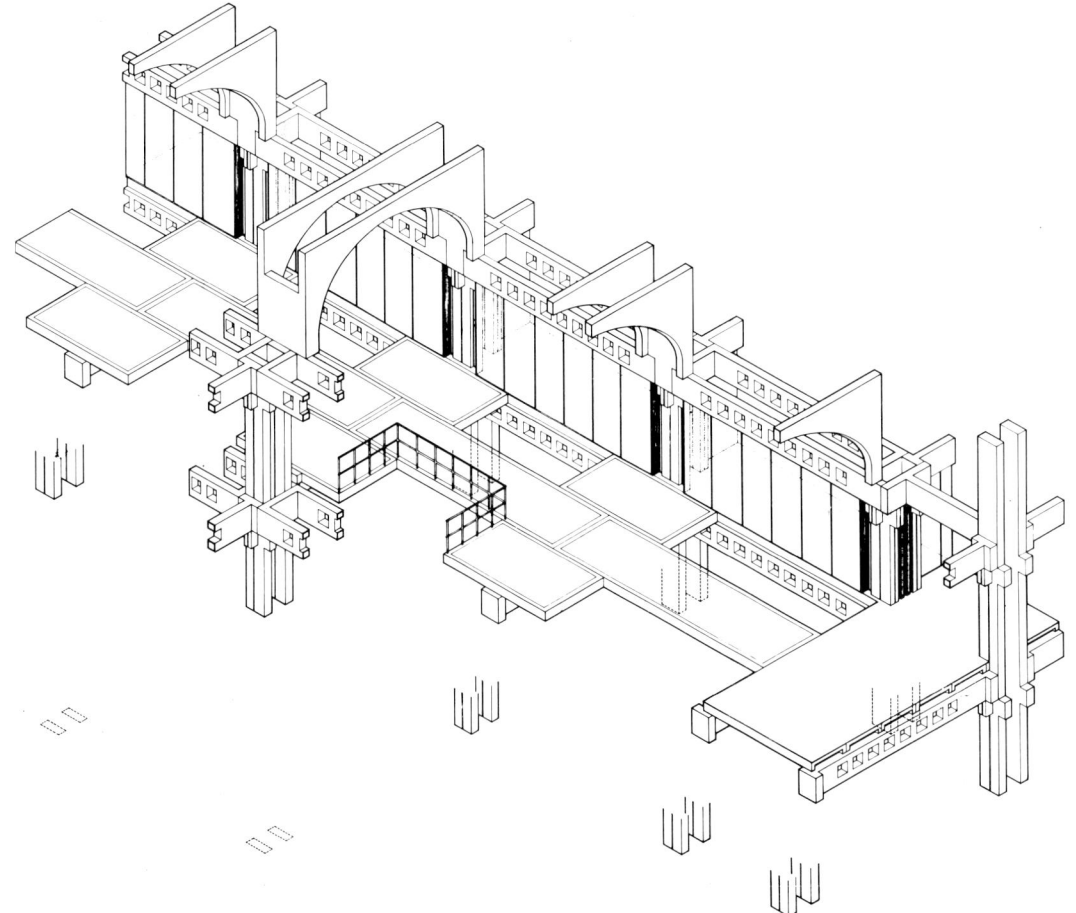

VITTORIO GREGOTTI
&
GINO POLLINI
Science Departments at the University of Palermo 1969-84

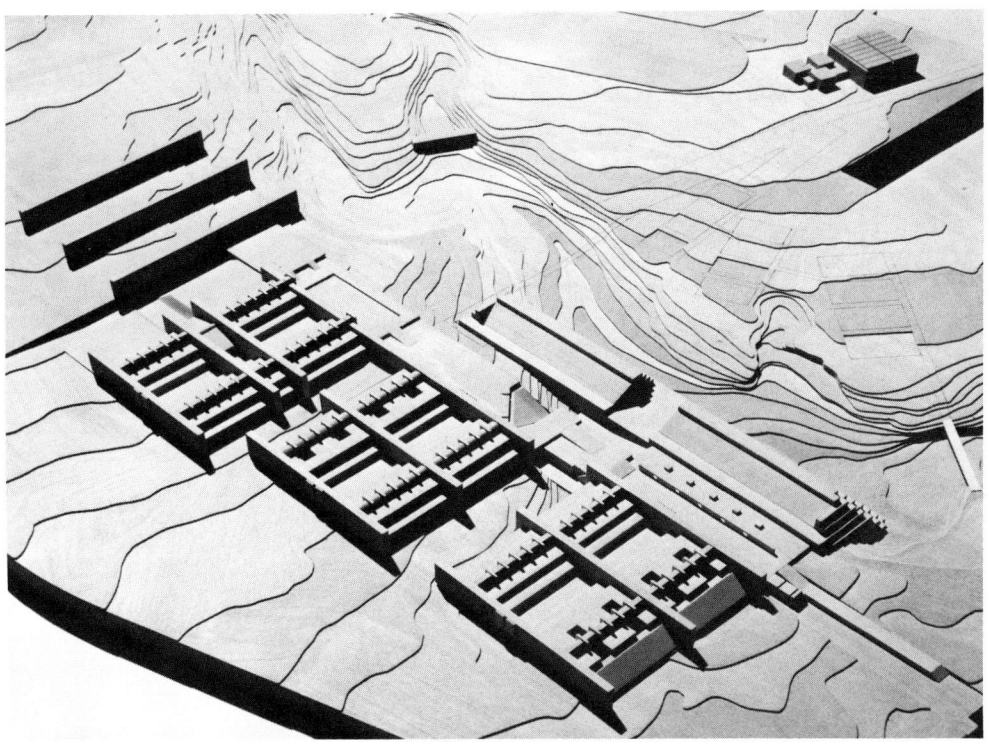

MODEL

The new science departments are located on a site in the Parco d'Orleans which abuts directly onto the historic centre of Palermo between Vias Brasa and Altofonti and existing buildings belonging to the University and the Polytechnic. The project as a whole involves the construction of new departments of Chemistry, Physics and Biology and, in a later phase, Mathematics and Geology. The maximum scope for expansion is 325,000 m^2; to this should be added 65,000 m^2 of general service buildings and student accommodation, and a total of 10,000 m^2 of connecting elements (parking spaces, squares etc). In addition, there are to be linked sports facilities, most of them outdoors, but some 10,000 m^2 in reserve indoors.

The complex of science departments is arranged on the axis of the present Viale delle Scienze and laid out around a set of three elongated pedestrian precincts on different levels. All the science departments abut onto the precincts, and the collective services for the student residences are aligned along them. The squares are orientated to make full use of the geographical lie of the land, which will be left unchanged as far as possible: the sports facilities will be developed on the far side.

The three squares are arranged on three different levels which follow the natural rise of the land. The first stage is 54 m above sea-level with numerous entranceways and connections to the collective services. The second, at 59 m, is designed as a hanging garden connected with the first square by an outdoor theatre whose arrangement follows the natural shape of the terrain. The third is set at 61 m above sea-level, and is envisaged as a pond to be constructed in front of the entrances to the departments of Mathematics and Geology.

Vehicles will run along a level below the pedestrian squares, following the route of the Viale delle Scienze and joining the new Via Brasa after completing a circuit of the whole system. This will serve the complex at every point from below as well as preserve the precious natural setting of the area.

Each department consists of two connected blocks, one essentially intended for teaching preliminary courses, the other for advanced courses and research. Each of these blocks will be developed on two floors, and will also have a basement level for parking and services. The basic module for both construction and installations of each block is 7.20 × 7.20 m. In addition to its research block, the Physics department will have a workshop along the axis of the block once the second phase of construction has been completed.

The vertical bearing elements are composed of a prefabricated double pillar (with an interaxis of 7.20 m both ways) which permits vertical passage of the conduits and utilities – electric power lines, compressed air, gas, water pipes, distilled water supply, ventilation shafts etc. These can run horizontally and are open to inspection under the prefabricated ceilings which are shaped to allow the continuous horizontal arrangement of the conduits in both directions.

This is the first earthquake-proof prefabricated and precompressed structure of any importance to be built in Italy.

Collaborators: Spartaci Azzola, Renzo Brandolini, Camilla Fronzoni, Hiromichi Matsui.

GENERAL VIEW FROM THE COUNTRYSIDE

THE DEPARTMENT OF CHEMISTRY

INTERIOR OF THE DEPARTMENTS

INTERIOR OF THE DEPARTMENT OF CHEMISTRY (ALL PHOTOS MIMMO JODICE)

ROB KRIER
Houses 7 and 16, Block 31, Linden-/Ritterstrasse, Berlin
1984

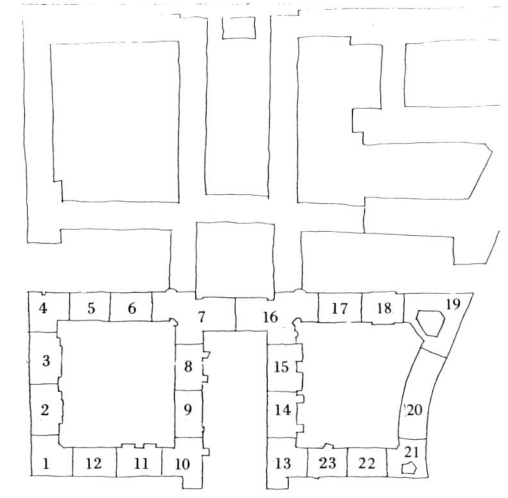

KEY
1,5,8,11 BANGERT, JANSEN, SCHOLZ, SCHULTES
6,10,13,15 BERNZMULLER, WORNER
2,3,23 FEDDORSEN, V HERDER & PARTNER
4,18,20 GANZ, ROLFFS

KEY
7,16 R KRIER
9,12,14,21 LIEPE, STEIGELMAN, BRANDT, HEISS
17,19,22 MULLER, RHODE

SITE PLAN

PHOTO COLLAGE VIEWS OF THE BLOCK FROM NORTH AND SOUTH (PHOTOS UWE RAU)

HOUSE 7 EXTERIOR

HOUSE 16 EXTERIOR (PHOTO PAPADAKIS)

HOUSE 16 FROM INTERIOR OF BLOCK

MOORE RUBLE YUDELL
Parish of St Matthew Episcopal Church
1983

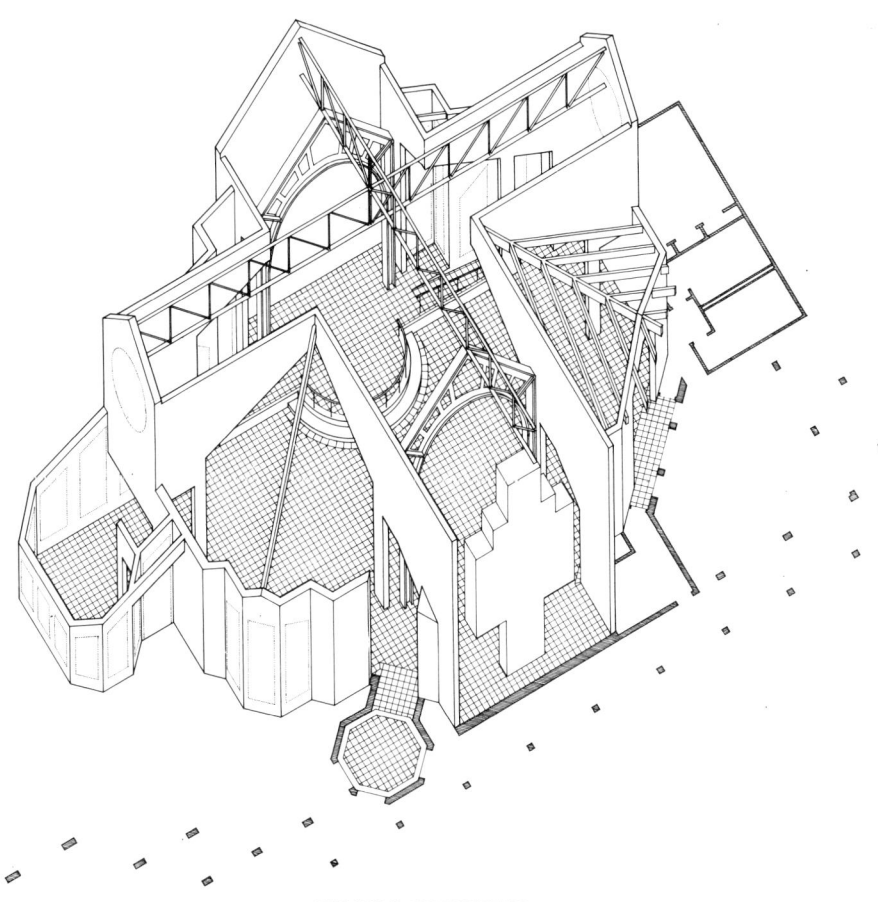

CUT-AWAY AXONOMETRIC

The Parish of St Matthew viewed the destruction of its church by fire in 1978 not simply as a loss, but as the opportunity to bring the church community together in the act of building anew. The Vestry gave us the exciting and frankly intimidating charge of involving the parish fully in the planning and design of the church. Further, the schematic design had to be approved by a two-thirds vote of the parish.

In a series of four monthly workshops, we invited the members of the congregation to collaborate with us and our consultants in decisions ranging from siting the building to determining its size, facilities, layout and budget. More than two hundred parishioners participated in this process and the schematic design gained approval of 87% of the congregation.

The workshops evolved as a forum in which diverging views were synthesised. Many parishioners wanted – for acoustic and liturgical reasons – a lofty symmetrical church with a minimum of glass and wood. An equally vocal group spoke out for a more informal and rustic building with intimate seating, views to the old prayer garden, extensive use of wood and a close relationship with the benign outdoors of Southern California.

The building evolved in close response to these issues as the workshop participants modelled the options. The traditionally configured nave and transept intersect a large hipped roof reminiscent of a more rustic Californian architecture. The roof is carved away to preserve favourite trees and create courtyards and a cloister for meetings, small services and quiet meditation. The shape of the roof was carefully studied for viewing from the surrounding hills. The walls are of structural steel frame with four inches of plaster for acoustics. To accommodate the desire for wood without sacrificing acoustics, a system of wall battens and wainscotting was developed. A three-inch thick wood deck was stiff enough to pass the acoustics test. Windows are minimised in the nave, but are located to frame views of the prayer garden. The construction of thick mullions and glazing reduced the loss of reverberation. A small chapel was made specially transparent to connect it with the outside.

Passing under low and informal porches one enters through a glass narthex to a lofty formal nave. Here liturgical processions are framed by arches of ornamented steel which in turn carry the major structural supports, a crossing of two steel trusses. The formal seating of more than 350 congregants is made intimate by its curved plan which allows everyone to be within seven rows of the altar. Energy-conscious parishioners suggested operable skylights at the ridge. These skylights and the building volume obviate the need for air conditioning, while the climate allows for minimal heating. The exterior of the building is stucco with expansion joints composed to recall but not mimic the 1920s half-timbered stucco of the nearby Founder's Hall.

We feel the success and excitement of the building lies in its demonstration that the open participation of a community can produce a building as sensitive to its time and place as any effort of the architect alone. The building can be a specific creation of the community while the architects, as partners, lose none of their importance as makers of form, place and ritual.

Collaborators: John Ruble (Project Manager); J Timothy Felchlin (Associate Project Manager); Robert Flock, Andra Georges, Shinji Isozaki, Peter Zingg (Project Staff); Jim Burns (Planning Consultant); Tina Beebe (Colours/Interiors); Campbell and Campbell (Landscape); Richard C Peters (Lighting); Kurily and Szymanski (Structural Engineer); Meskell and Sons (General Contractor); Jane Marquis (Stained Glass); Purcell Noppe & Associates (Acoustics).

EAST ELEVATION

SOUTHWEST ELEVATION

WEST ELEVATION

KEY
1 NAVE
2 CHOIR
3 ALTAR
4 NARTHEX
5 BAPTISTRY
6 CHAPEL
7 CHOIR PRACTICE
8 ACOLYTES
9 LIBRARY
10 CLERGY
11 SACRISTY
12 CLOISTER
13 BELL TOWER
14 COURTYARD
15 COVERED WALKWAY
16 MECHANICAL

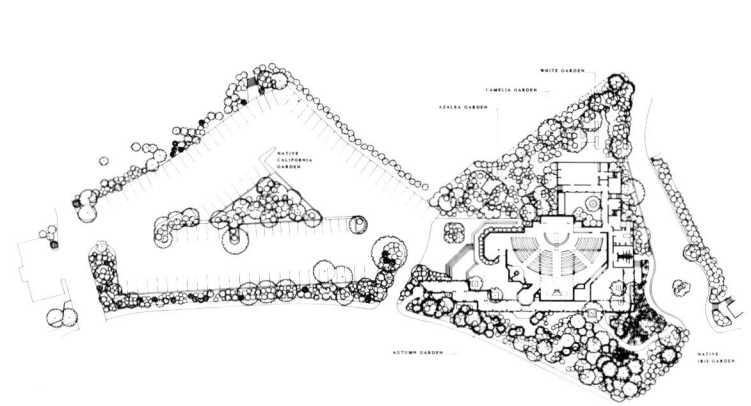

SITE PLAN (LANDSCAPE BY CAMPBELL & CAMPBELL)

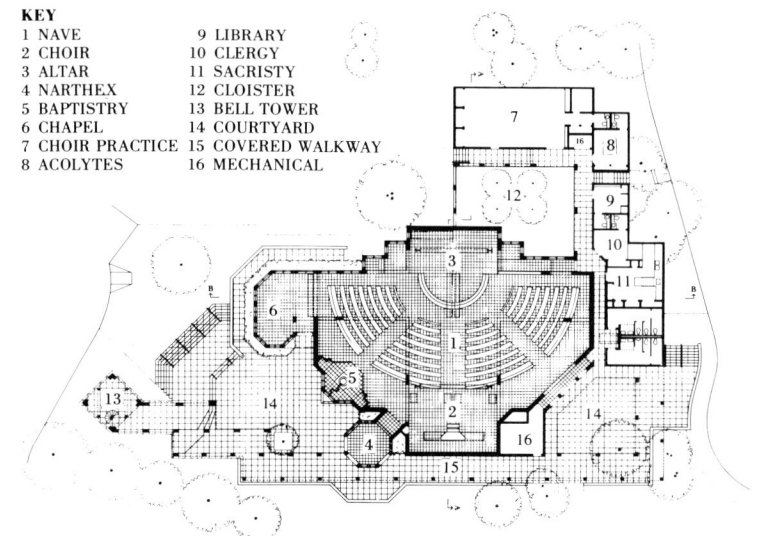

GROUND FLOOR PLAN

VIEWS FROM THE SOUTH AND SOUTHEAST AND NAVE (PHOTOS TIMOTHY HURSLEY © THE ARKANSAS OFFICE)

PERSPECTIVE OF THE MATTHAIKIRCHE AND THE SQUARE

PERSPECTIVE OF THE FUTURE COLONNADE AND THE NEW SQUARE

PERSPECTIVE OF THE MATTHAIKIRCHE

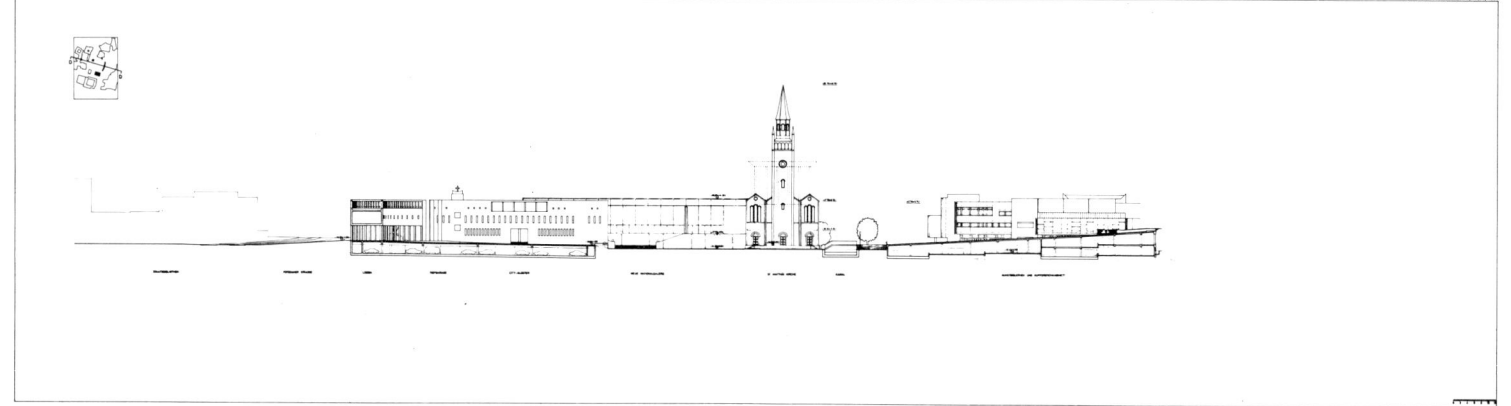

EAST-WEST SECTION, 2ND PHASE, 1984

HANS HOLLEIN
Kulturforum, West Berlin
1983-87

The Kulturforum is located next to the Tiergarten, north of the Landwehrkanal. It consists of a large square which links buildings of different significance and architectural character. Hans Scharoun's expressionistic Philharmonic, Mies van der Rohe's classical National Gallery and the historic classical Matthäikirche form the overall context. Three new buildings, a monastery for the Protestant church, an exhibition pavilion, a glass-enclosed colonnade at the east side of the square, and a waterway are the most important new design proposals. The waterway will be connected with the nearby Landwehrkanal to define and to link the square and the surrounding buildings. A monorail system leads directly to the Kulturforum on the east side.
Completion is expected in 1987.

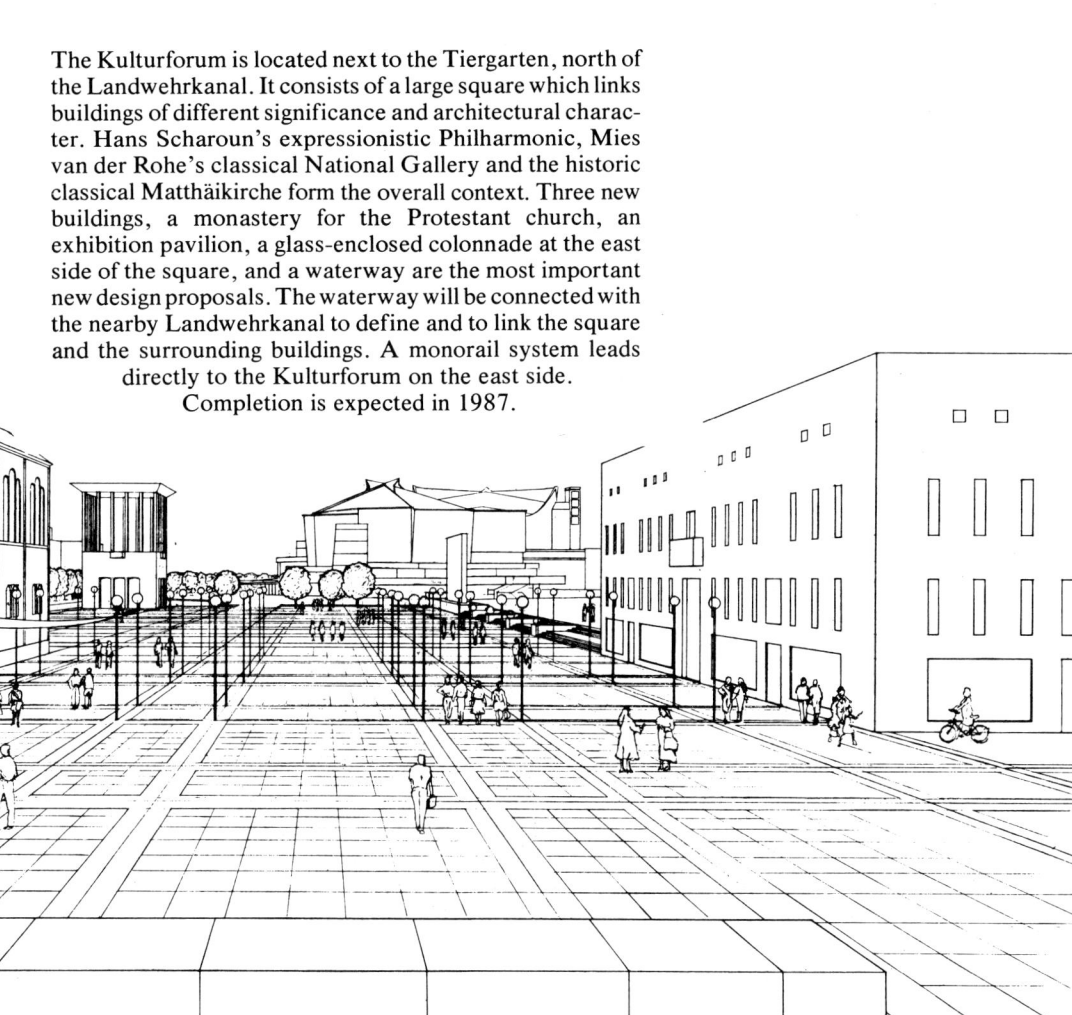

PERSPECTIVE OF THE FUTURE CHAMBER MUSIC HALL AND EXISTING PHILHARMONIC HALL BY SCHAROUN

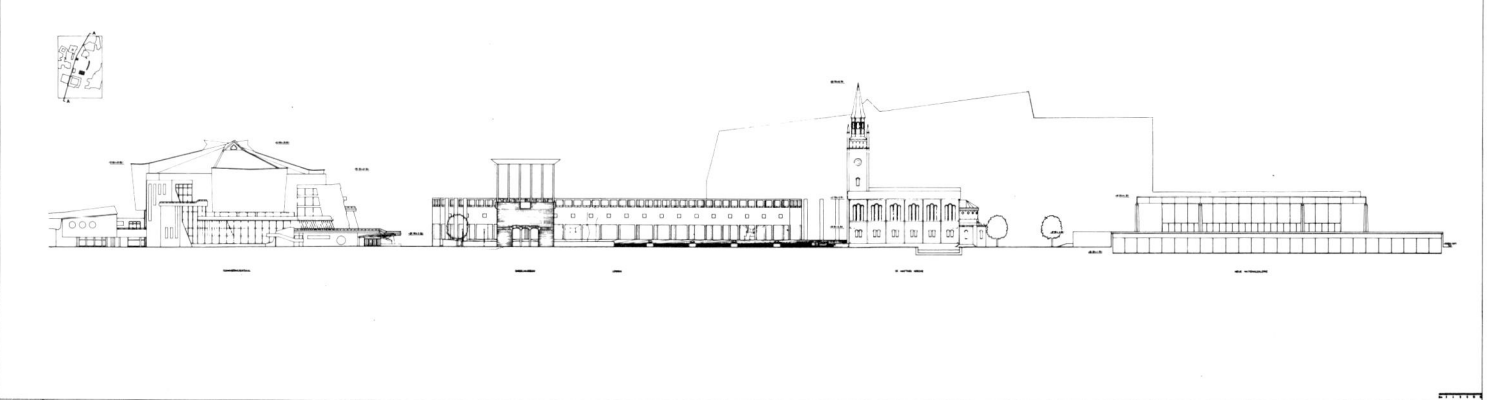

NORTH-SOUTH SECTION, 2ND PHASE, 1984

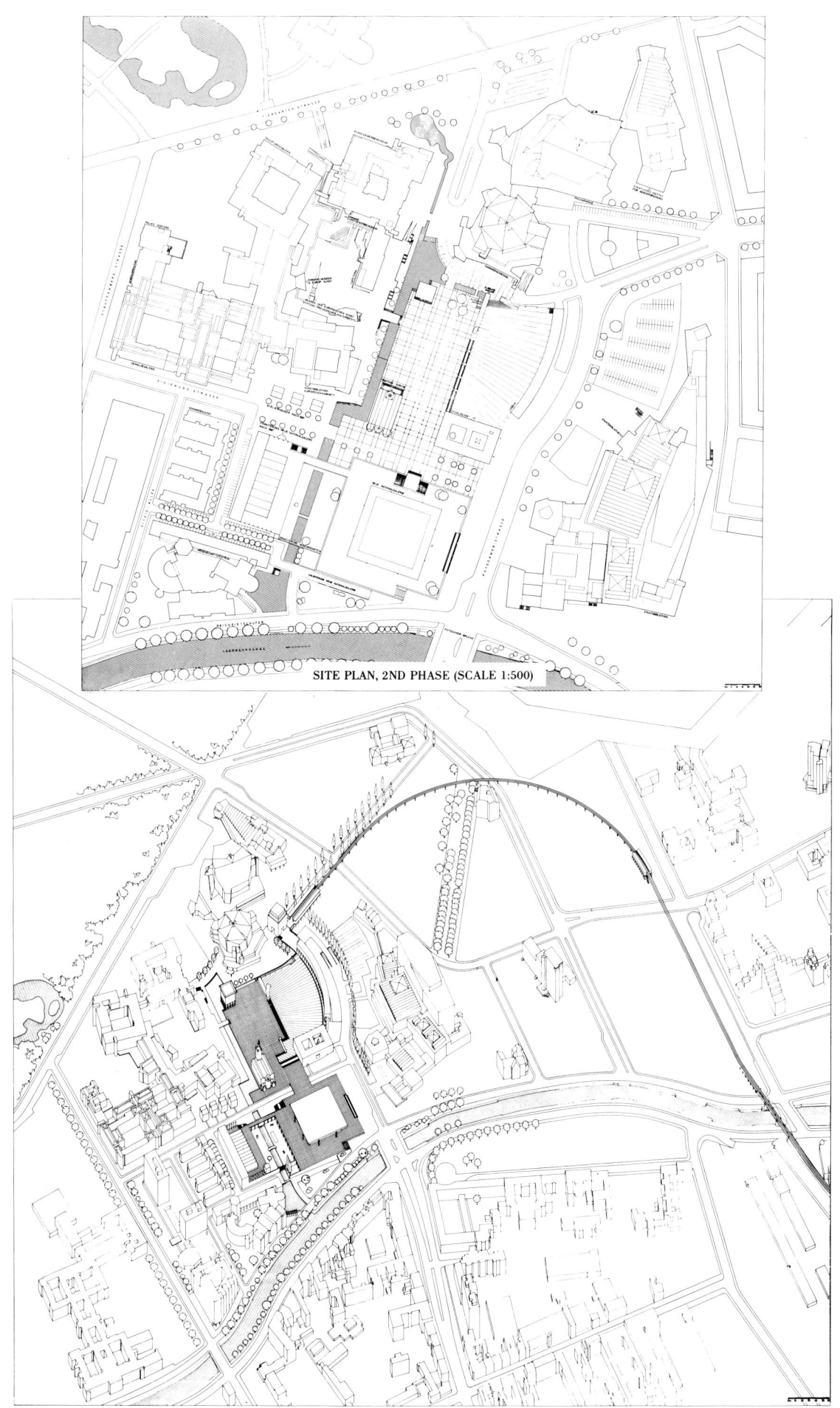

SITE PLAN, 2ND PHASE (SCALE 1:500)

AXONOMETRIC OF COMPETITION ENTRY, 1983 (SCALE 1:1000)

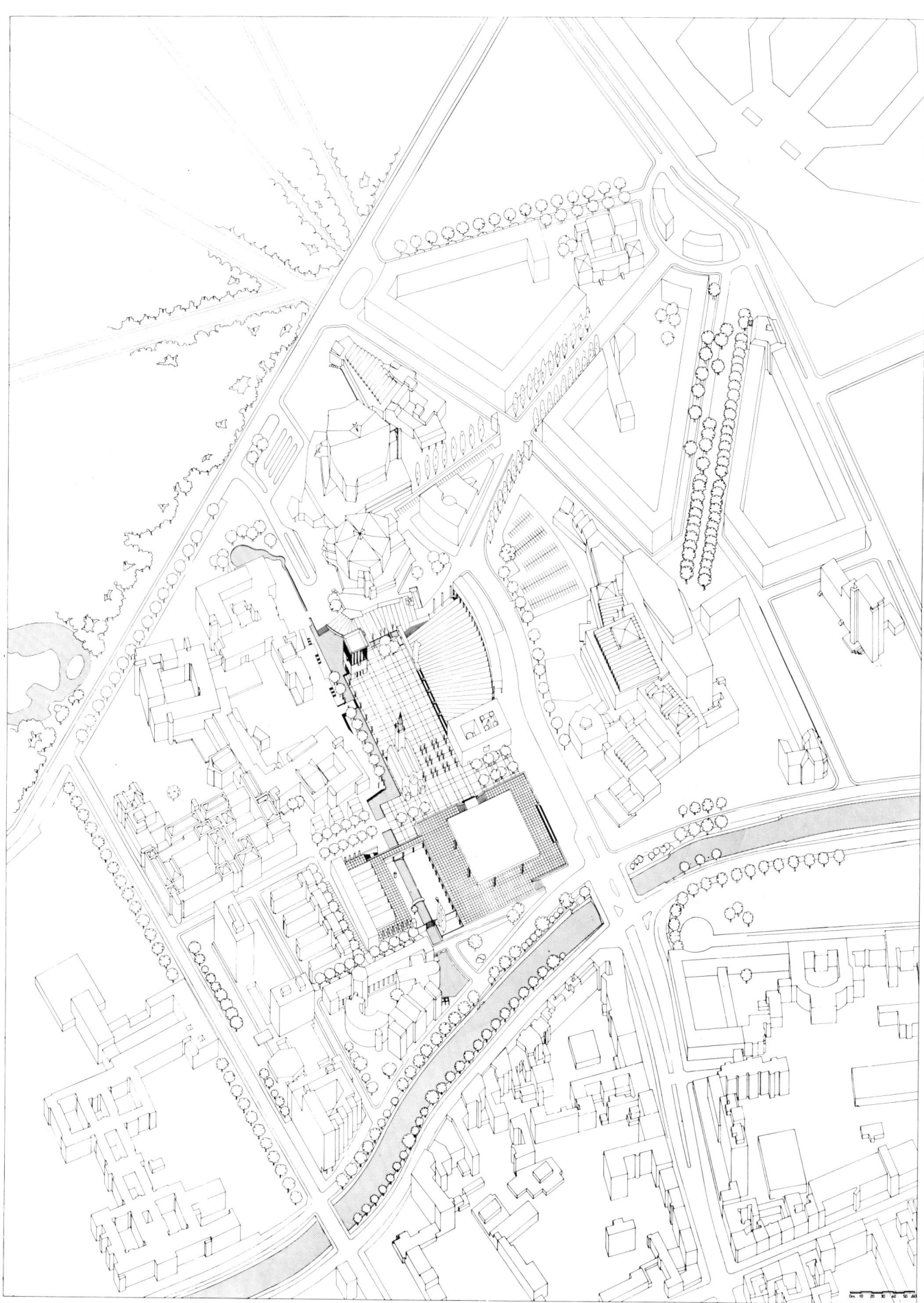

AXONOMETRIC 2, 2ND PHASE, 1987 (SCALE 1:1000)

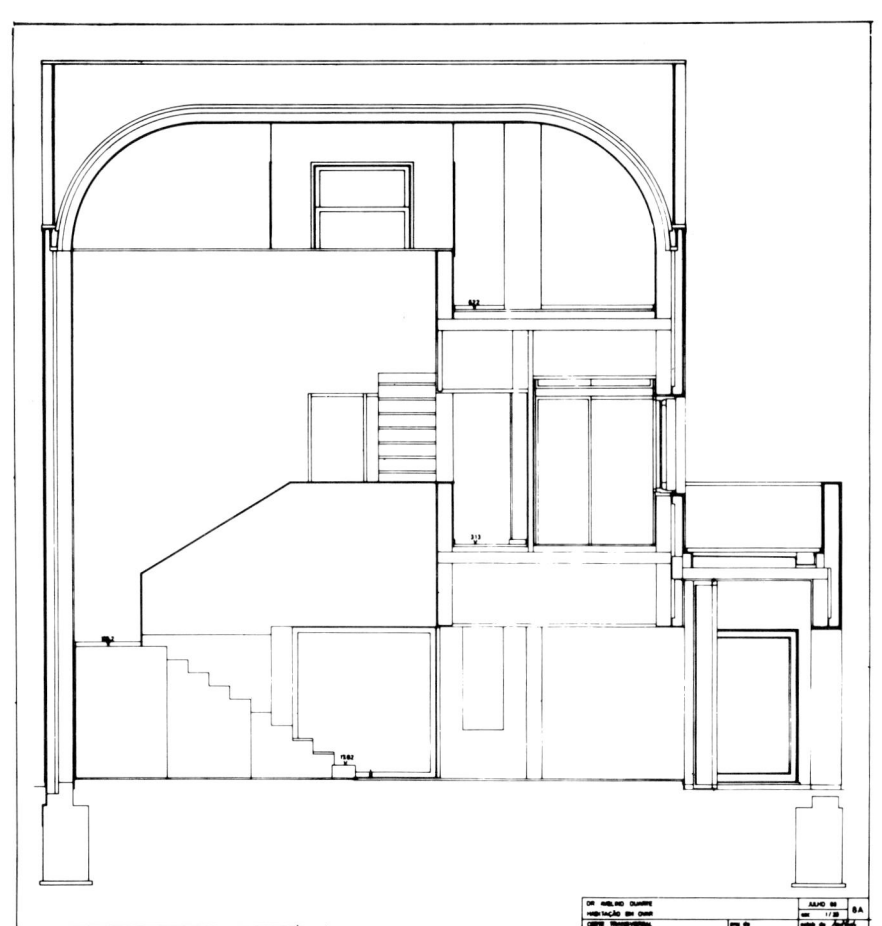

CROSS SECTION

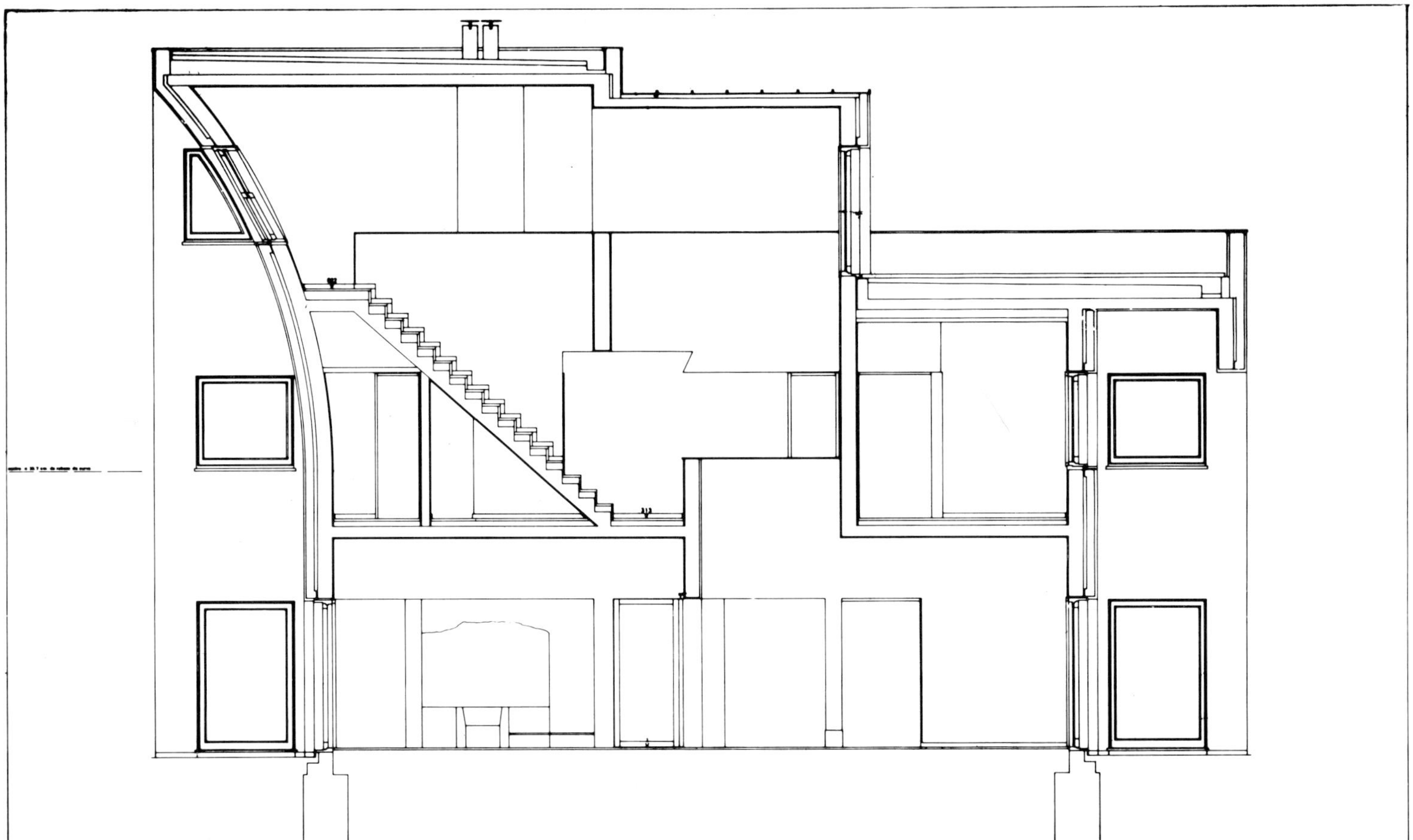

LONGITUDINAL SECTION

ALVARO SIZA
Avelino Duarte House
near Ovar
1984

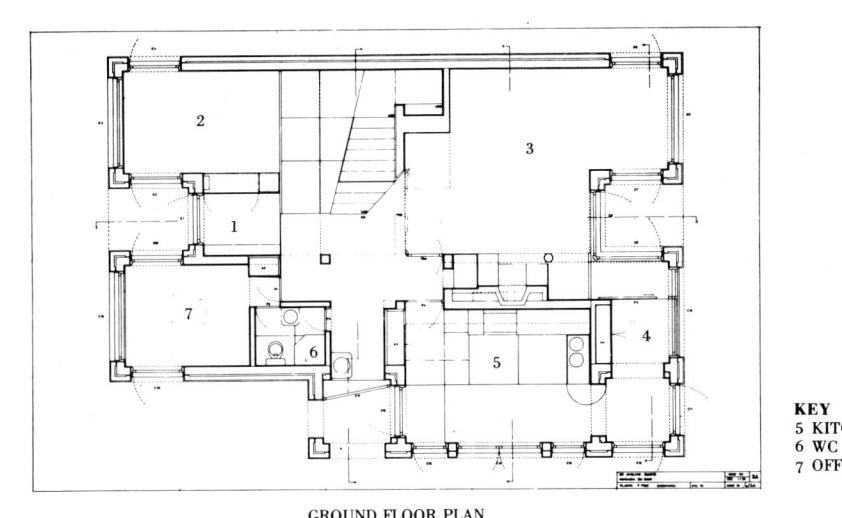

KEY
1 HALL
2 VESTIBULE
3 LIVING ROOM
4 SERVICE

KEY
5 KITCHEN
6 WC
7 OFFICE

GROUND FLOOR PLAN

The house is sited on the Portuguese coast, on the outskirts of the town of Ovar. A solicitor and his family will live in it.

ELEVATIONS

PERSPECTIVE VIEW OF THE LOGGIA

PERSPECTIVE SECTION OF THE FOYER AND LOGGIA

JAMES STIRLING, MICHAEL WILFORD & ASSOCIATES

Cornell University Performing Arts Center
1982

The Performing Arts Center for the teaching of theatre arts is also a performance centre for the university, city and region. It is prominently sited on College Avenue, close to the bridge over Cascadilla Gorge, reinforcing this entrance to the campus and the link between the university and collegetown communities. The design comprises a group of buildings connected by a loggia appropriate to the park-like character of the gorge.

The building is planned to permit two phases of construction. The first phase would establish the building's presence on College Avenue, and includes a plaza, loggia, proscenium theatre, foyer and dance studio. A walled garden could temporarily occupy the site of the second phase building. The second phase would contain additional performance spaces, including a flexible theatre, studios and offices, and could be constructed independently of an existing first phase building.

A pavilion and plaza signal the entrance to the new complex. The pavilion contains an advance ticket office, a servery for refreshments on the plaza, and provides a shelter for the adjoining bus stop. Two seminar rooms are located in its upper level and it is crowned by an illuminated sign announcing current productions.

Entry to the new building is through the loggia, a promenade approach with spectacular views across the gorge. Part of this loggia is glass-enclosed to provide an all-weather lobby leading to the central foyer. A spiral stair at the west end of the loggia descends to grade allowing access from adjacent footpaths.

The foyer located at the centre of the building connects all major spaces, encouraging interaction between theatre, dance and film groups, and bringing guest artists into close contact with students and faculty. This foyer opens to the loggia enabling audiences in the intermissions to stroll in and out to take the view. Foyer and entrance are overlooked by a late sales ticket window.

Proscenium and flexible theatre are entered on either side of the foyer. The proscenium theatre seats approximately 500 on a main level and two balconies. Fixed seating has centre and side aisles and the balconies have loose seats. These balconies wrap around the auditorium bringing audience and performers together in a small-scale theatre room. An observation gallery (for teaching purposes) is at the rear of the auditorium. The forestage can adapt to orchestra pit or thrust stage as required. Staircases on both sides connect the balconies with the foyer. The flexible theatre has multiple entrances to permit arena, thrust, alley or proscenium configurations. The audience seated on adjustable platforms varies from 140 to 180 people. Studios and classrooms adjoin the flexible theatre.

On the level below the entrance are the dance performance studio and forum. The dance studio (below the proscenium theatre) accommodates 180 people, with multiple choice of audience and performer relationships. Bleacher seating allows the floor to be cleared for teaching. The forum accommodates 100 people in fixed seating and is suitable for films, lectures and small theatre productions.

Administration and faculty offices are located in a mezzanine around the upper part of the flexible theatre with internal access from a balcony overlooking the foyer. An entrance from the footpath around Sheldon Court gives external access to the administration, studios and graduate offices occupying the top floors.

The green room, which can be opened to the entrance foyer for receptions and parties, is at the same level as the proscenium and flexible theatres. Below the green room are faculty showers and locker rooms which can double as dressing rooms for visiting performers. Above are student dressing rooms, lockers and showers. A backstage stair connects these areas with the performance spaces.

Production support spaces are grouped on the south side of the building with access through soundproof doors onto the proscenium and flexible theatre stages. A central area in the scene shop has 25 feet of headroom for scenery construction and painting. Truck access at shop floor level allows vehicles to be driven on to the performance stages if required. A costume shop is located below the stage house.

The existing footpath on the old trolley route will be diverted towards the gorge through a garden between the new building and Cascadilla Hall. Steps will connect the existing footpath along the gorge with the new plaza on College Avenue.

The project can be built independently of further development on the College/Dryden/Cascadilla block. Existing parking lots will be re-graded and landscaped, and provision has been made for service access to the Performing Arts building behind Sheldon Court. Access from the parking lot is via a new footpath around Sheldon Court to the plaza on College Avenue. En route, activities in the scene shop can be viewed through windows in the building.

The building footprint (both phases) is within University boundaries and back from the edge of the gorge. However, removal of undergrowth, diseased trees and utility poles would allow better views of the gorge, campus and Lake Cayuga.

External materials have been chosen to relate to adjoining University buildings. The primary facades to College Avenue and the gorge are surfaced in limestone with brick string courses. Other facades are of brickwork with limestone string courses. The loggia has a slate roof and other sloping roofs are clad in metal.

Construction phase documents were completed in March 1984 and bids invited in April 1984. Building construction should take two years and be completed in the spring of 1986.

Collaborators: Wank Adams Slavin Associates – New York (Associate Architects); Severud-Perrone-Szedgezdy-Sturm – New York (Structural Consultants); Hanscomb Inc – Toronto (Cost Consultant); Artec Consultants – New York (Theatre Consultant); Jennifer Tipton – New York (Lighting Consultant)

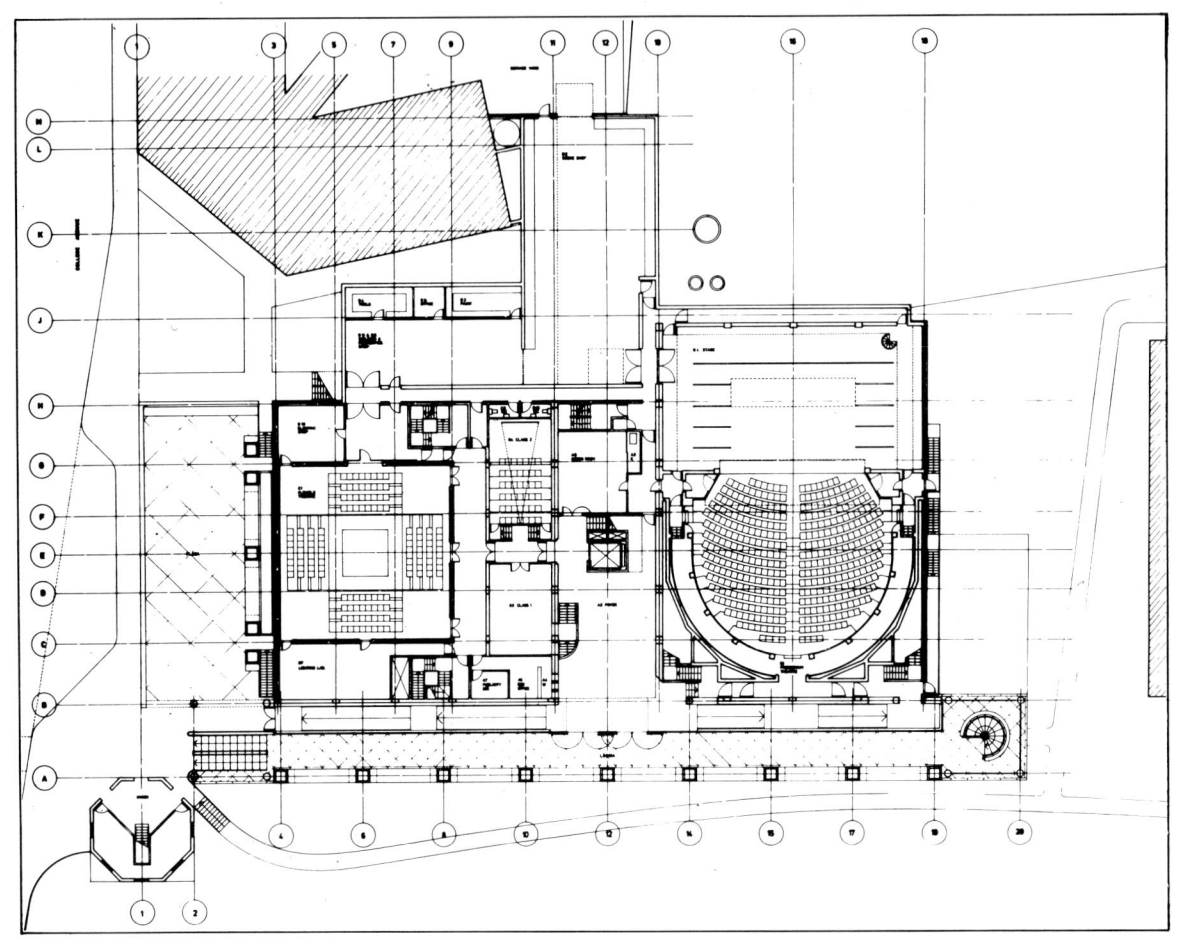

GROUND FLOOR PLAN

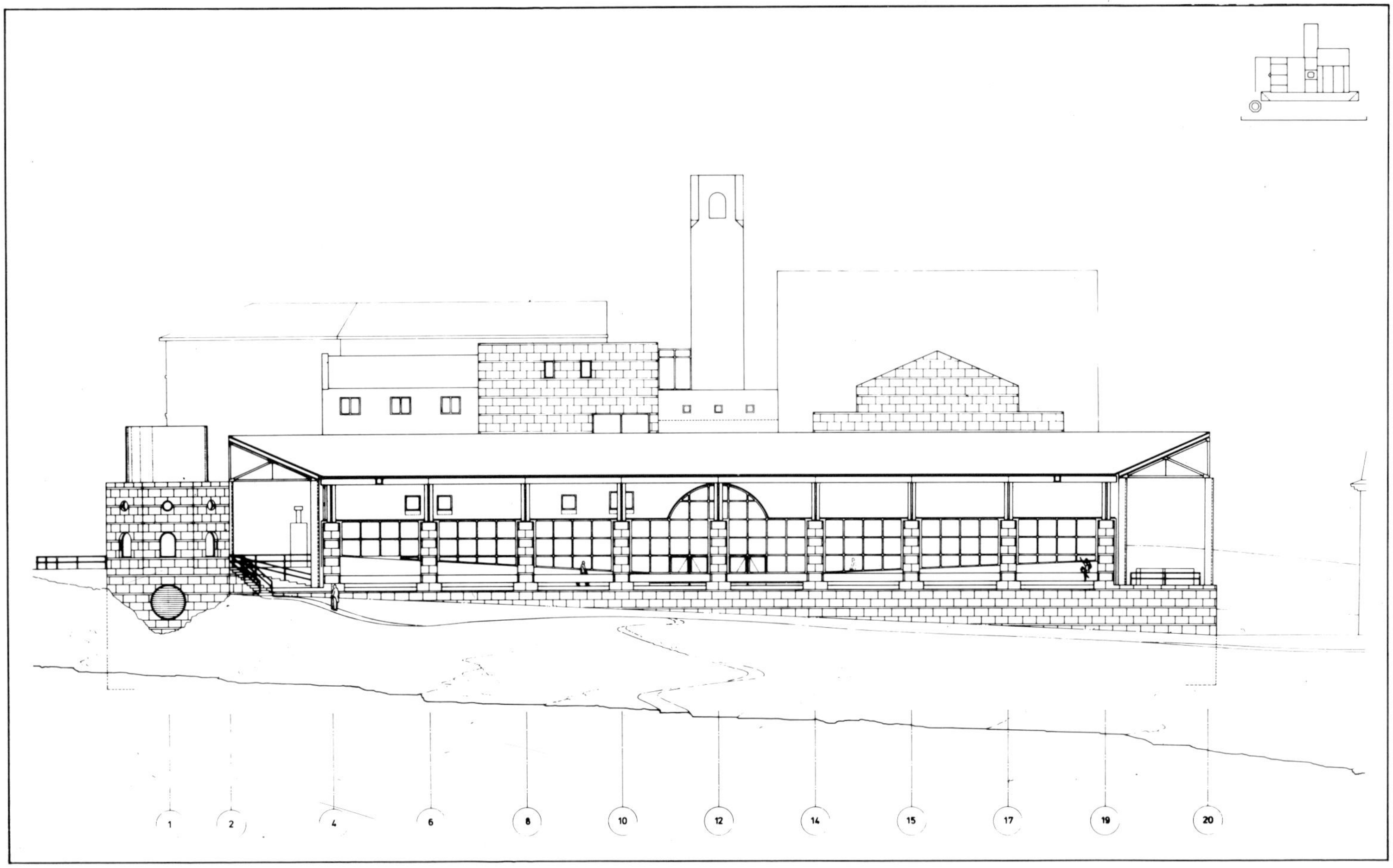

NORTH ELEVATION

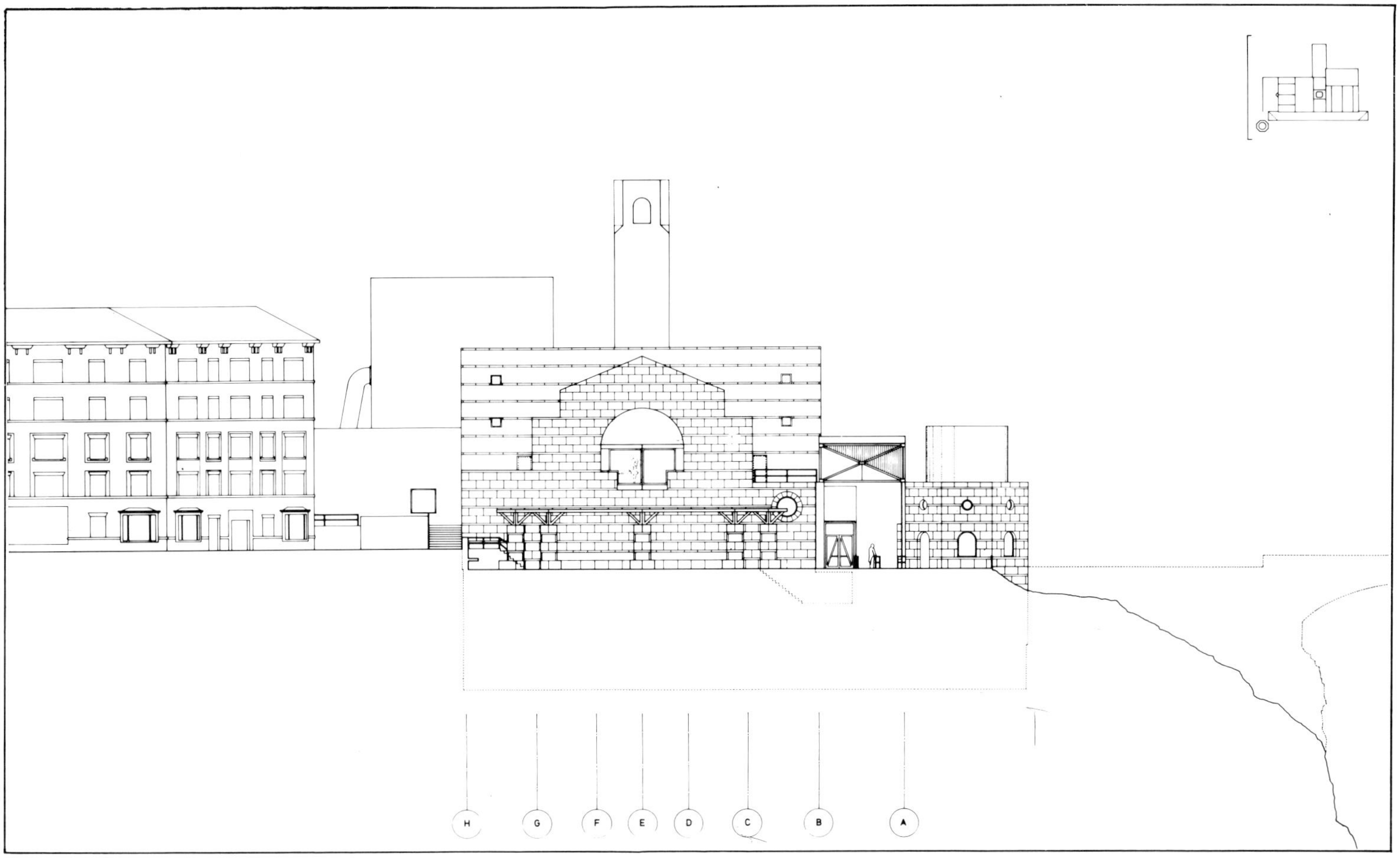

EAST ELEVATION

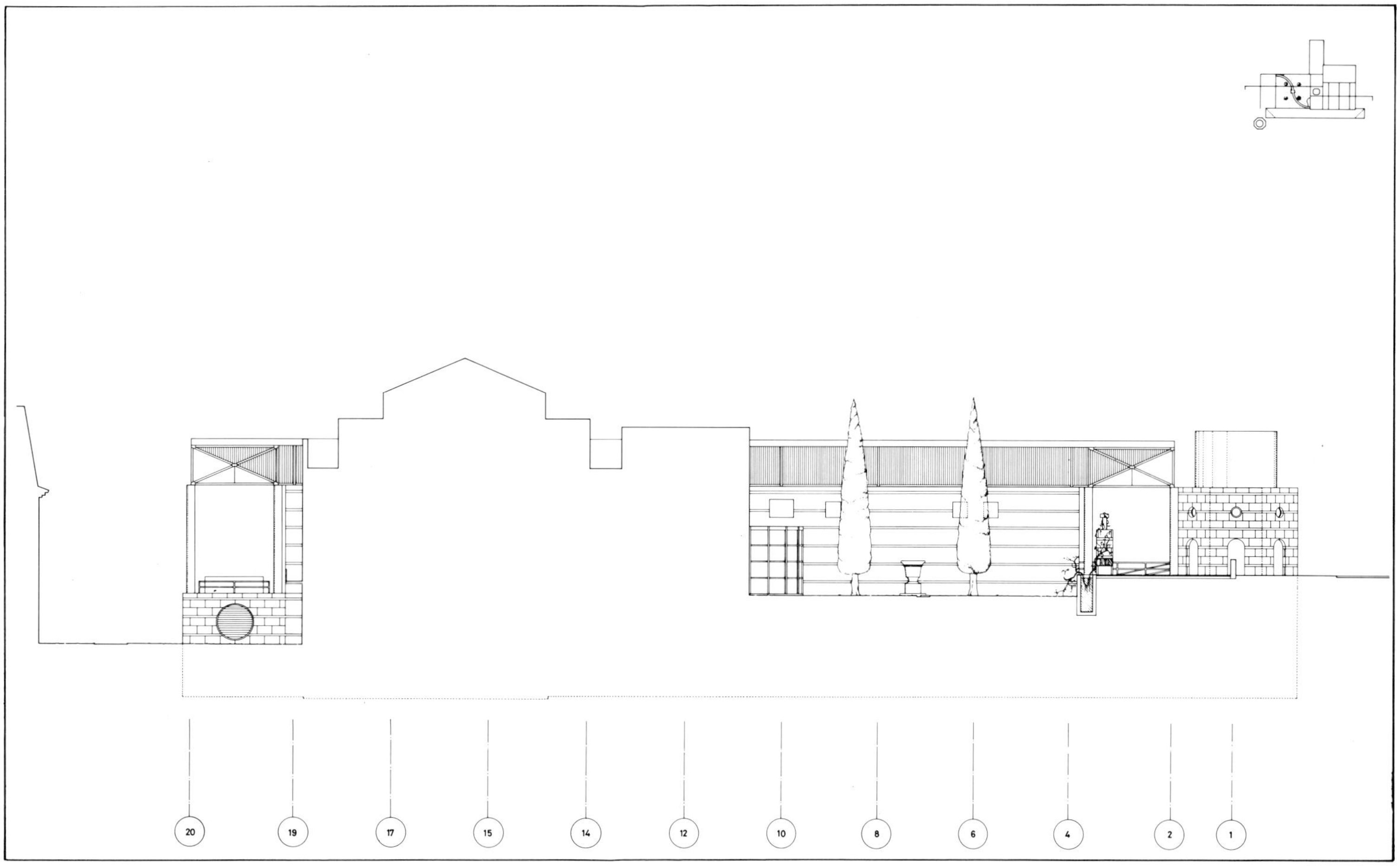

SOUTH ELEVATION

65

MIGUEL ANGEL ROCA
Projects for the City of Cordoba, Argentina
1979-80

THE SHADOWS OF THE CATHEDRAL, PLAZA DE ARMAS

The correct relationship between architectural typology and urban morphology could dilute the false antithesis between architecture and urban design and planning in the recovery of the discipline as urban art.

Qualitative, even historical, distinctions between modern architecture and architecture of the past are not admissible. The latter is as modern as the former in the measure of its articulation of the present productive context (pluralist freedom, content).

The existing architectural product must be dehistoricised to recover its value, not as regards form but mainly as regards content. Our production, however, must be historicised to be converted into a constituent part, an integral part of socio-economic changes and relations.

Just as there is no progress in art, so there is no progress in architecture from either an aesthetic or a functional viewpoint because its practice belongs to an orientation or cosmovision that embraces disciplinary specificity in the context of wider cultural interpretation (social, political, economic and so on).

As regards certain contemporaneous conditions, one can and must ask what is the relation of architecture to productive conditions: whether it accepts them to a certain degree, in a reactionary way, whether it attempts to modify them or whether it aspires to a revolutionary elaboration.

The two irreducible institutions – street and square; the three structurising elements of the existential image of space – nodes, places or monuments; routes, roads, links between arrival and departure spots; and the most anonymous urban fabric – districts, areas or neighbourhoods: they are all the unique basic models for the recovery, reconstruction or materialisation of the public domain which is the basic task of urban art (architect-urbanism).

THE SHADOWS OF THE 'CABILDO'

PLAZA DE ARMAS

PERSPECTIVE VIEW OF THE PEDESTRIAN MALL

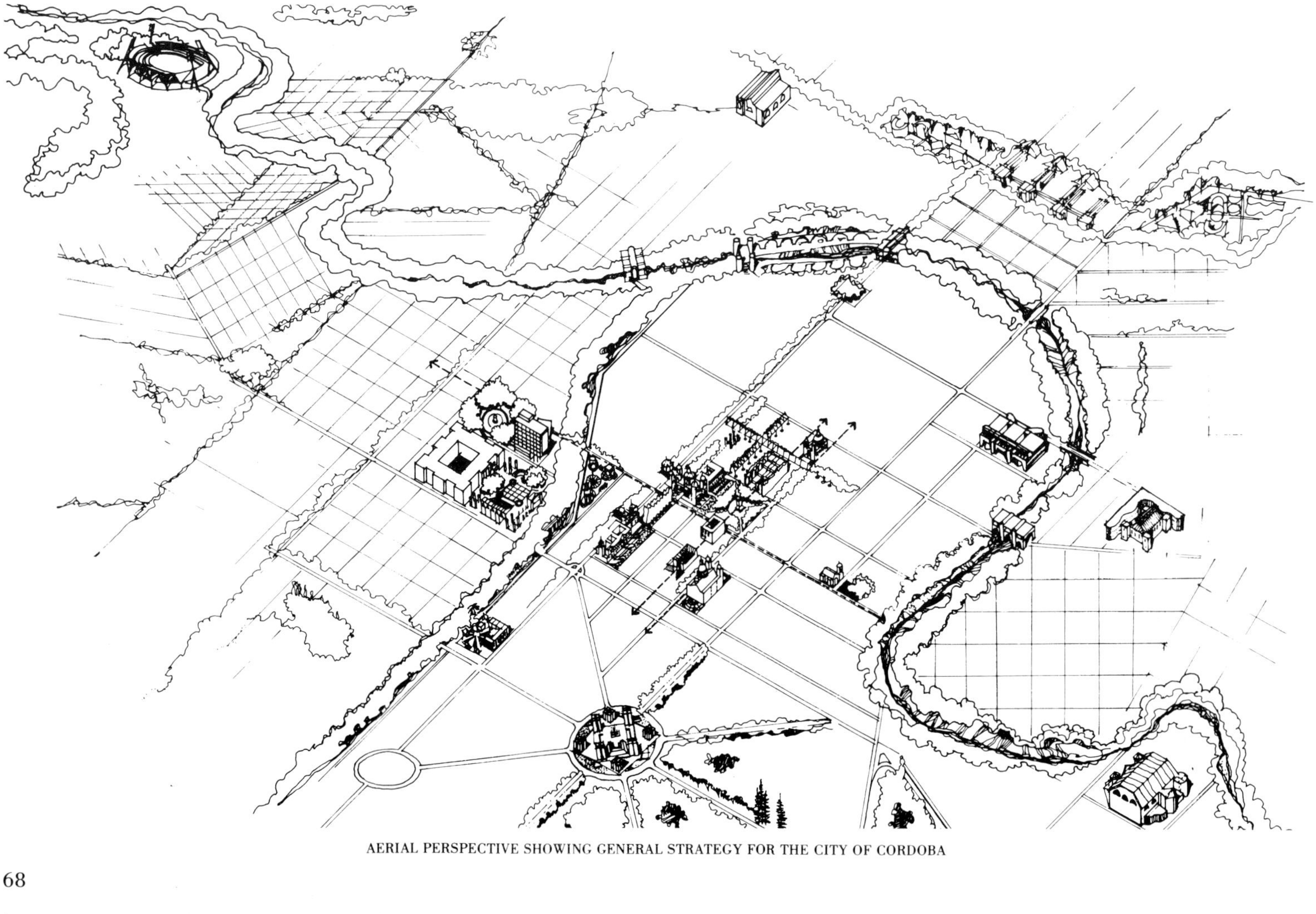

AERIAL PERSPECTIVE SHOWING GENERAL STRATEGY FOR THE CITY OF CORDOBA

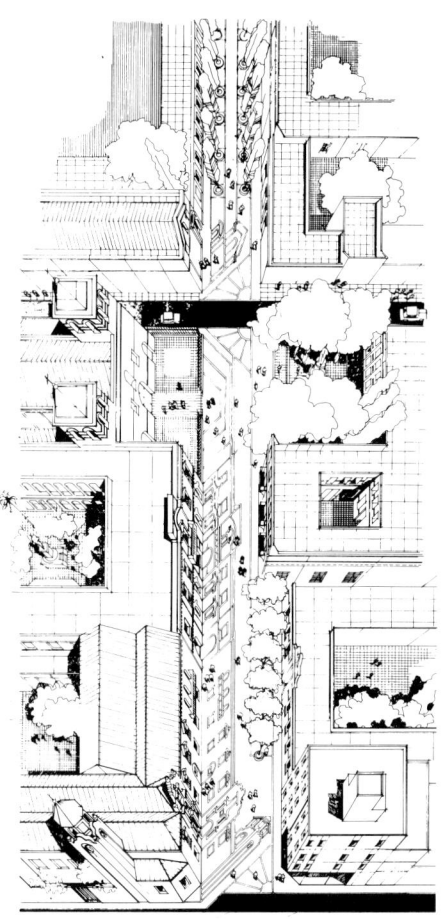

AERIAL PERSPECTIVE OF UNIVERSITY MALL

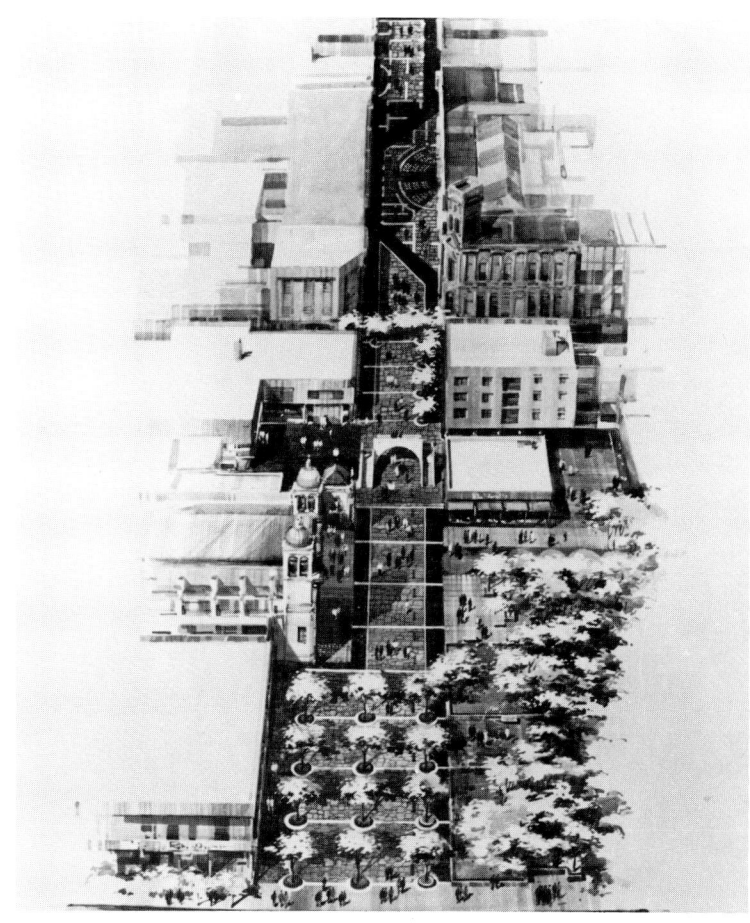

AERIAL PERSPECTIVE OF PEDESTRIAN MALL, OBISPO TREJO AND RIVERA INDARTE

THE SHADOWS OF THE UNIVERSITY AND CHAMBER OF DEPUTIES, PEDESTRIAN MALL

VIEW FROM THE SOUTHEAST

EAST ELEVATION (ALL PHOTOS PETER AARON © ESTO PHOTOGRAPHICS INC)

ROBERT A M STERN
Residence at Chilmark, Martha's Vineyard 1979-83

ENTRANCE AND GABLE

Set on one of the Island's highest sites, commanding water views in three directions, this shingled house with its gently flared hipped roof, dormers, bay windows, and subsumed porches continues the language of traditional seaside architecture that emerged in the 1870s and has ever since defined for many summertime living along the New England shore. At the entrance the roofline is interrupted by a large gable containing the asymmetrically located front door and circular window lighting the generously proportioned stair behind. On the opposite side, the hipped roofs are distended to provide a second-storey balcony overlooking the principal view.

Collaborators: Roger H Seifter (Associate-in-Charge); Alan Gerber (Assistant).

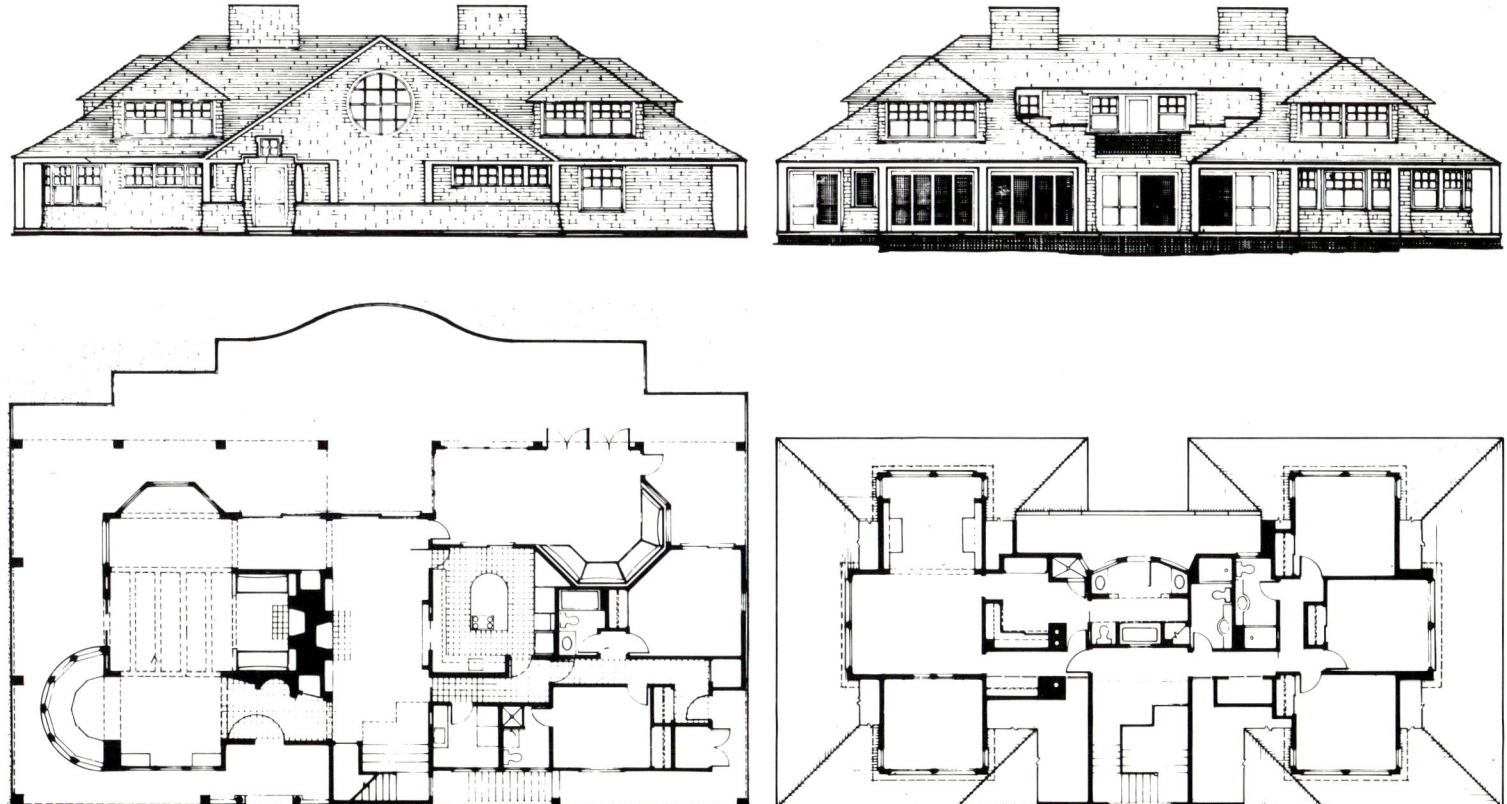

EAST AND WEST ELEVATIONS, GROUND AND FIRST FLOOR PLANS

VIEWS OF THE EXTERIOR AND CAR PARK (PHOTOS THE ARKANSAS OFFICE)

TIGERMAN FUGMAN McCURRY
Knoll International Showroom
at Houston
1984

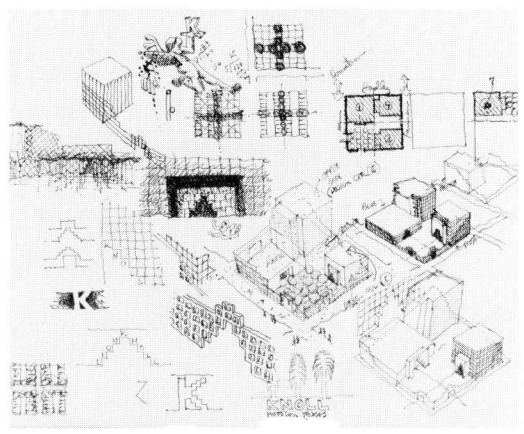

PLAN

Knoll International's new Houston showroom occupies a remodelled 1917 building of 15,660 ft² floor area in the 2300 block of downtown Houston between Main and Fannin streets. The recycling represents the first phase of a three-phase project to reinvigorate the entire city block of which the showroom is but one quadrant.

In the quadrant immediately adjacent to the showroom itself is an on-grade parking lot with four gateways so that the parking quadrant is thought of as an outdoor room. The showroom itself is translucent white glass gridded with baked red enamel mullions. Because one can see through the showroom, the solids and voids of the existing building become a perceivable memory on the new facade and a dialogue is created between the old and new. The interior of this one-storey building is tripartite in plan with the centre section 'pulled apart' so that the trace of the existing columns reveals the original concrete of the building. That part of the plan represents the showroom which is reflected on the outside white grid in dark grey. The intention is that as one enters the showroom space, one is thrust on-stage with the furniture both left and right acting as an 'audience'. Thus the spectator becomes the performer.

Stanley Tigerman (Principal in Charge); Robert Fugman (Project Architect); Margaret I McCurry (Interior Architect); Lee Stout (Interior Design); Ray Bailey Associates (Associate Architect); Ray Beebe (Structural Engineer); Wallace Migdal (Mechanical/Electrical Engineer).

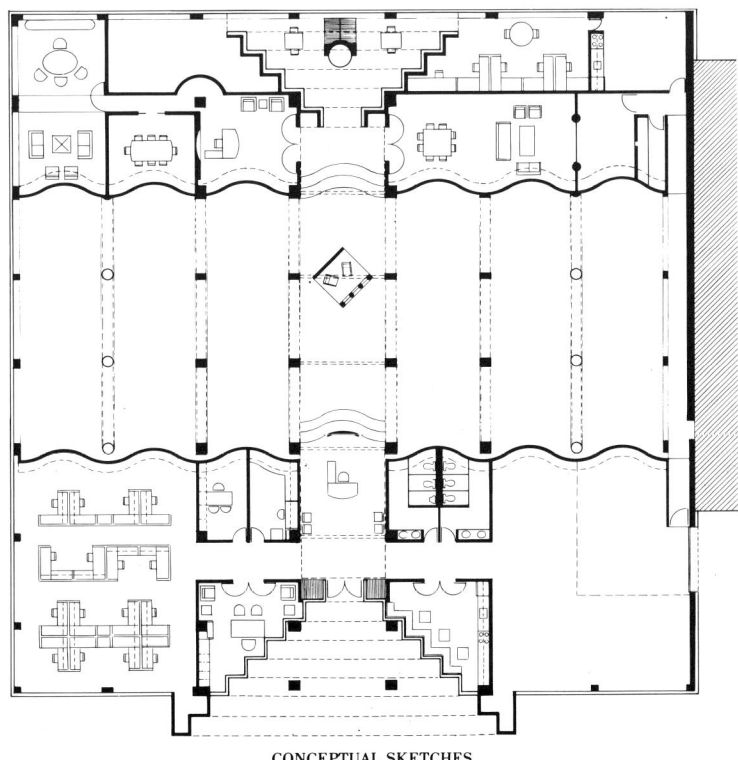

CONCEPTUAL SKETCHES

KNOLL INTERNATIONAL SHOWROOM, VIEWS OF THE INTERIOR (PHOTOS THE ARKANSAS OFFICE)

74

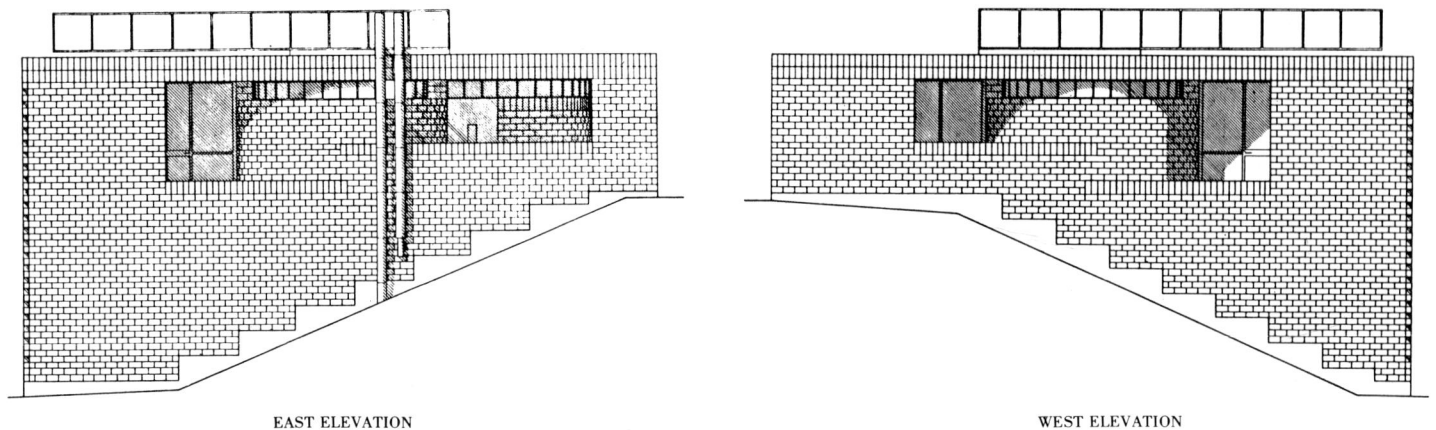

EAST ELEVATION

WEST ELEVATION

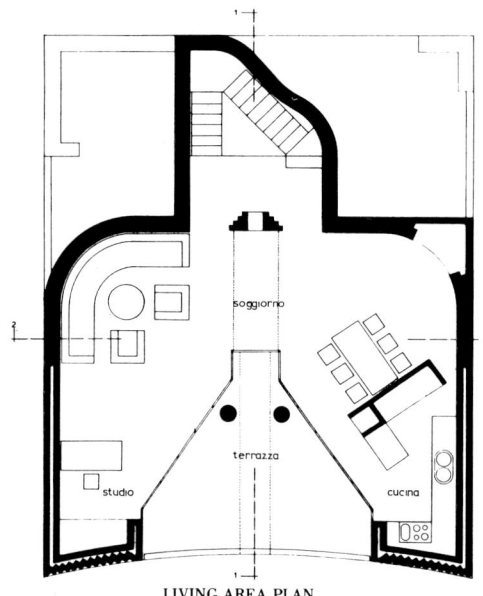

LIVING AREA PLAN

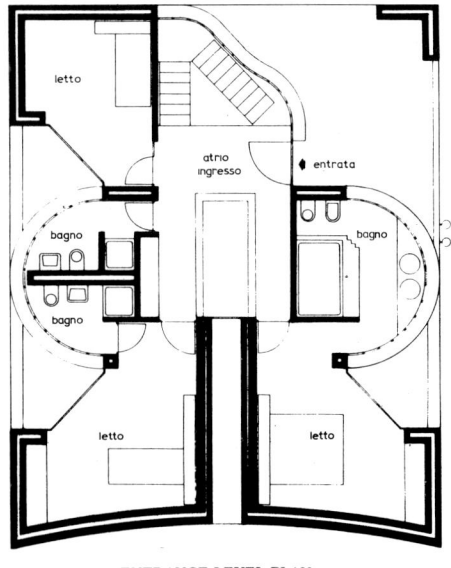

ENTRANCE LEVEL PLAN

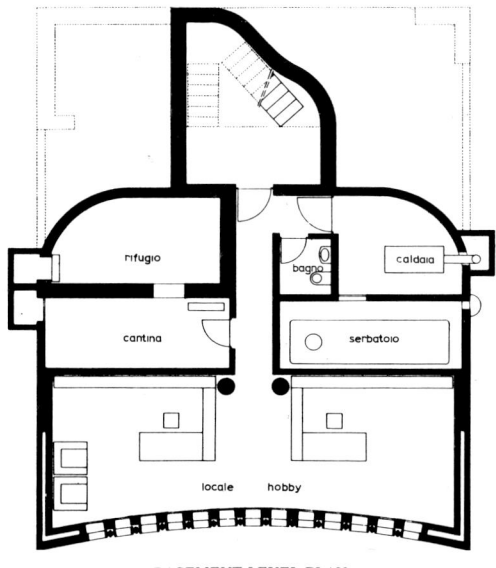

BASEMENT LEVEL PLAN

MARIO BOTTA
One-family house at Morbio Superiore
1983

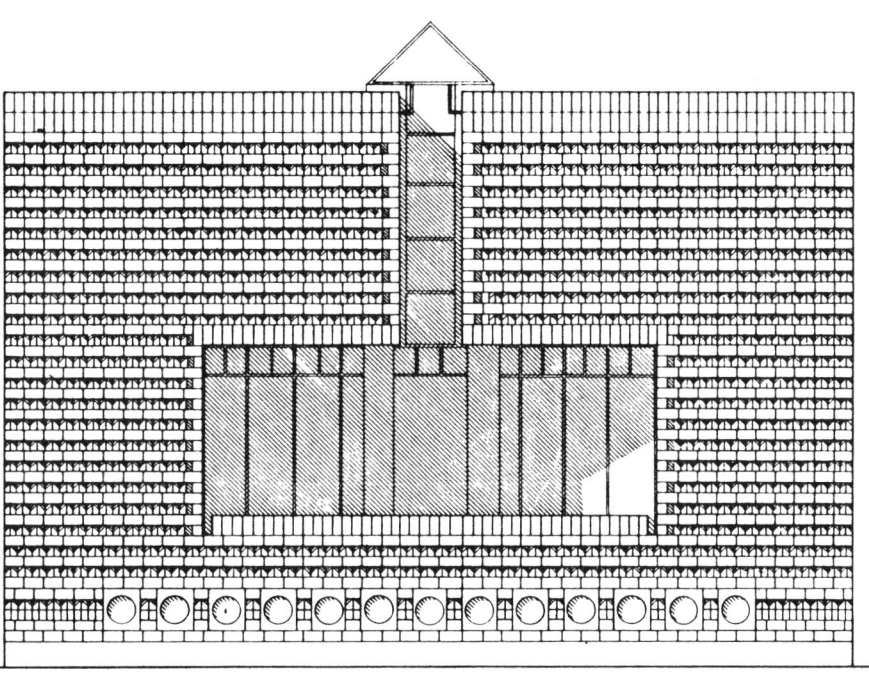

SOUTH ELEVATION

The nearly level tract of the hill is brusquely interrupted by a sudden descent towards the lowlands of Chiasse. The house, placed precisely at the point where this change happens, no sooner emerges from the level terrain than it confronts the valley, a precise sign in the landscape.

In fact, this slightly concave western facade is treated with alternating brick courses at a 45° angle, as already partly used in the house at Viganello. Here, however, the play of chiaroscuro is extended to the entire inner wall and accentuated by the silver-painted cement blocks. Along the east-west axis a skylight illuminates the deep cut crossing the entire structure and concluding in the great opening of the wall facing the valley. Off the rear loggia are the kitchen and living room, while on the upper level are the bedrooms open to lateral loggias with curved spaces for services. The entrance, preceded by a porch, is situated on this level.

The construction is realised in cement blocks with slate flooring and concrete ceilings. The internal walls are painted white with bolts outlined in black.

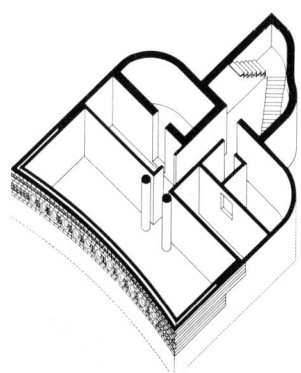 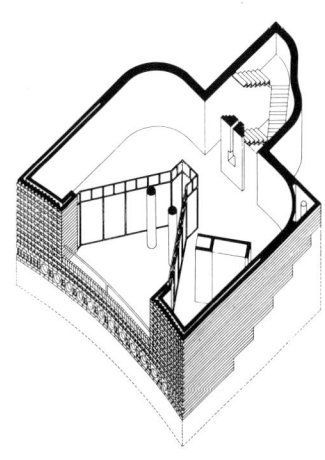 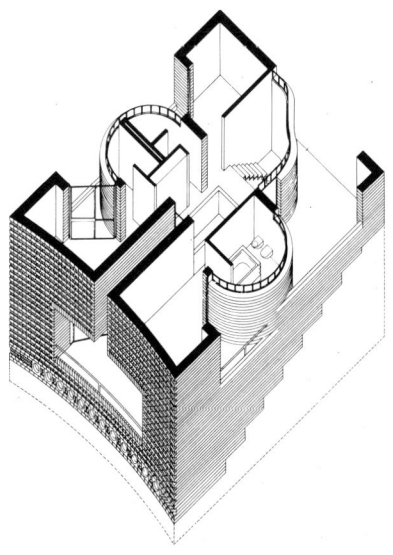

BASEMENT LEVEL, LIVING LEVEL AND ENTRANCE LEVEL CUT-AWAY AXONOMETRICS

VIEWS FROM THE NORTH AND SOUTHWEST

VIEWS OF THE ENTRANCE LEVEL AND INTERIOR

ALDO & HANNIE VAN EYCK
Restaurant and Conference Facilities for ESTEC, Noordwijk, the Netherlands 1984

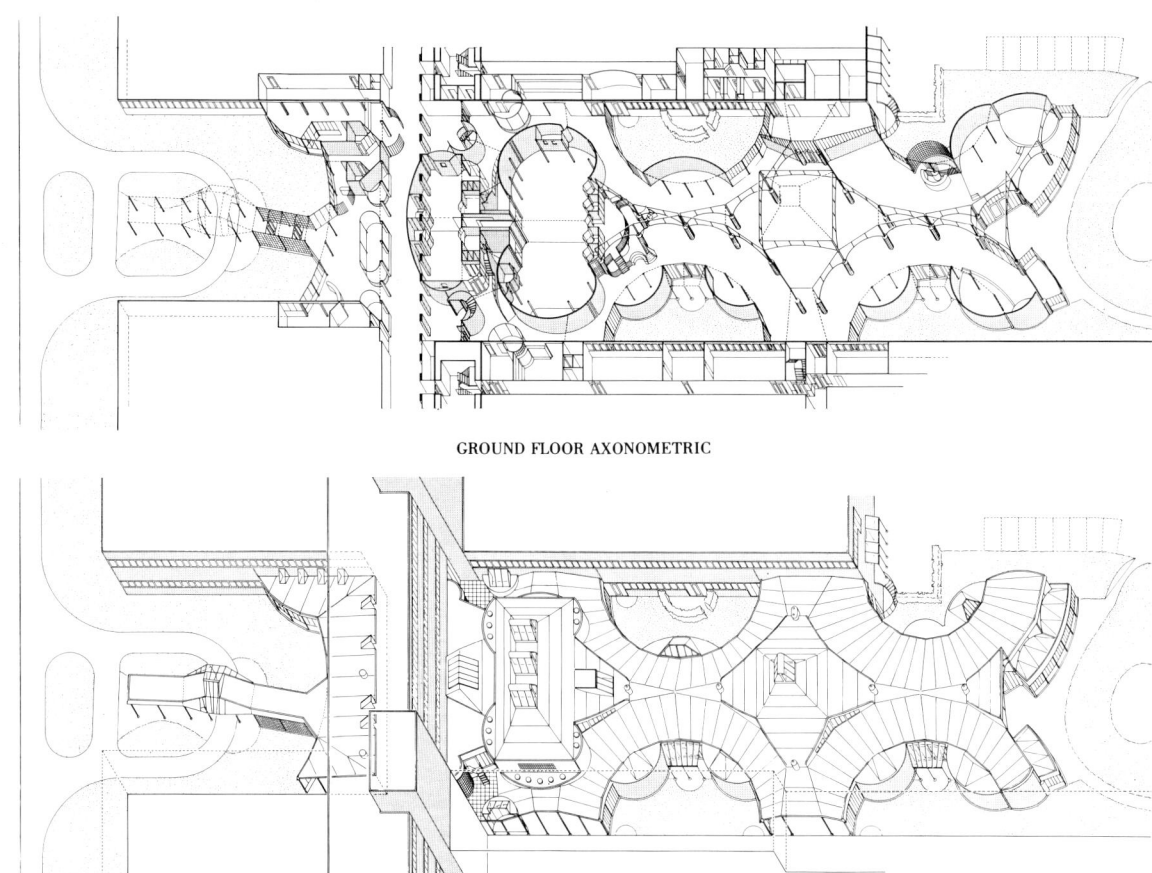

GROUND FLOOR AXONOMETRIC

ROOF LEVEL AXONOMETRIC

Since the present ESTEC (European Space Research and Technology Centre) building complex has no recognisable 'core' or centre of gravity, it seemed right to locate the new facilities, all of which have a more or less communal function, halfway down the main internal traffic artery on the ground floor and first floor immediately above it. By plugging the new building into the main block of the old one over not just one but two floors, ample daylight will enter from the stairwell into the previously closed and artificially lit interior thoroughfare. The two additional staircases leading up to the library and down to the toilets are open ones providing visual contact with activities on both floors.

The introduction of a new entrance with a reception, travel office, bank etc, at this point will emphasise the 'core' idea. These facilities, and the general opening up to daylight, sky and gardens on both sides are assets which will benefit not only those going to and from the new centre functions, but others too.

The curvilinear interior and exterior walls permit a compact linear organisation whilst sustaining a fluent spatial development and easy movement from place to place along the stem. The formal contrast vis-à-vis the existing structure is intentional, and old and new will together form a unity nonetheless.

As to construction and materials, only the two large conference/meeting spaces will have walls of masonry within a concrete structural frame; this will ensure good sound insulation. All of the rest of the building, ie the restaurant, kitchen and reading room library superstructure, will be of steel painted white with natural colour timber frames on the windows and doors, and horizontal and vertical infill panels and partitions both inside and outside. In order that each place may acquire its own identity, all curved hollow interior walls will be given a different, rather active colour.

Along the entire length of the new dining wing, doors open onto glass-covered exterior terraces and beyond these onto gardens. The restaurant will provide a considerable choice of seating positions, some orientated towards the outside, others more introverted. Curved screens will articulate the length of the restaurant and coffee bar corners.

The roof is the new building's most exposed feature. It holds the sequence of spaces together, transmits light from above and, when seen from the upper floors of the existing building, represents from the outside what occurs below it. The roofing material should therefore be aesthetically pleasing as well as durable – we suggest non-corrosive zinc or, better still, copper sheet.

In general, representational extravagance has been avoided. Rather, the construction, proportions and straightforward unadorned use of a small number of sound materials will convey what we believe to be the right congenial atmosphere: elegance without unnecessary luxury.

The varying height and irregular shape of the restaurant space are acoustically very favourable. With respect to their shape, the same can be said of the conference/meeting rooms.

Crawlways running along and under all 25 main columns will contain heating and ventilation ducts. Input and output will be via the hollow spaces inside the columns.

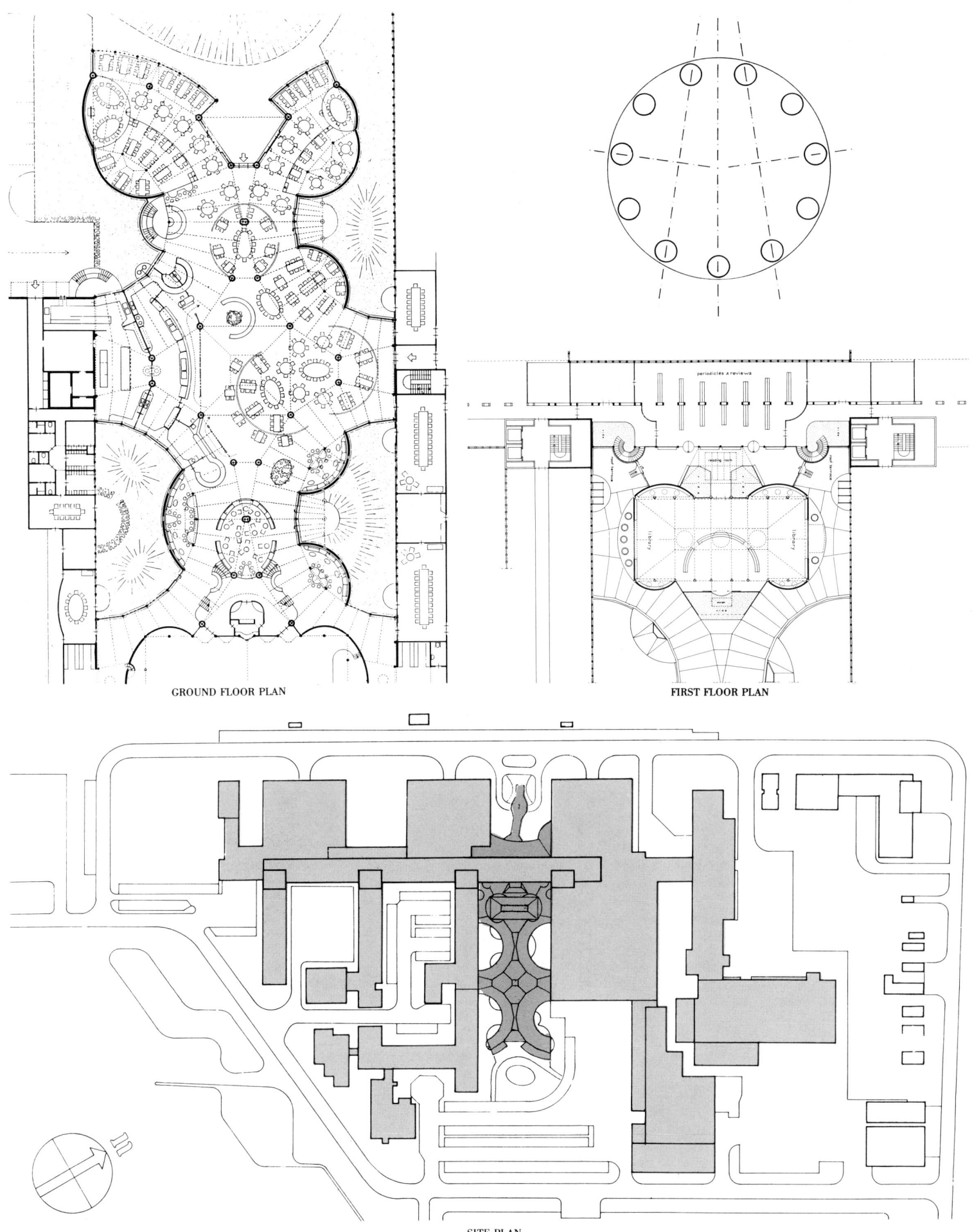

GROUND FLOOR PLAN

FIRST FLOOR PLAN

SITE PLAN

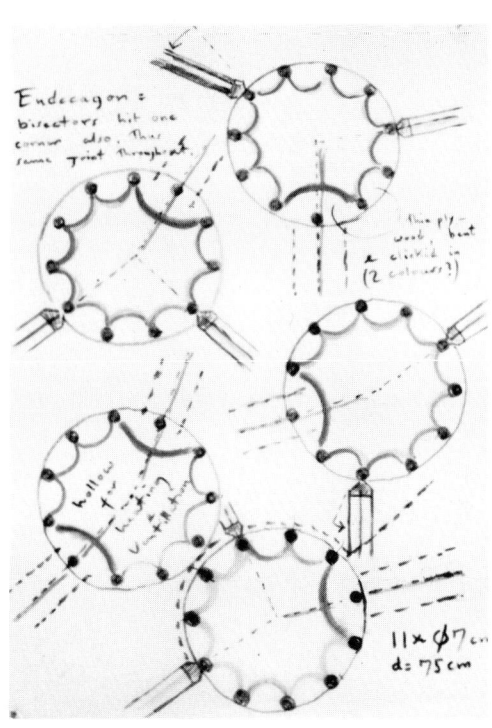

An Hendecagnoic proposal

The circular columns down the centre of the restaurant are made up of 11 steel tubes in a ring between two steel discs. The columns are squat: height 1.90 m, diameter 0.80 m, the distance between them 6.80 m. Inside, they contain heating and ventilation ducts. The hollow panels between the tubes are of thin plywood bent into position.

Hendecagons have angles which correspond to those of the building's principal construction. Moreover, like pentagons and heptagons they have sides opposite corners, so that in the case of the columns there is always a corner tube to terminate and hold a partition or wall. Segments of a column's circumference between two such partitions or walls are clearly articulated vertically by the number of intermediary tubes – one, two, three or four etc.

We like our hendecagons; they keep telling us that relevant – accurate – solutions often hide in what is still less obvious or unusual, but are simply waiting to become straightforward through application.

Fewer quotes and rather more hendecagonic enquiry might be a good thing!

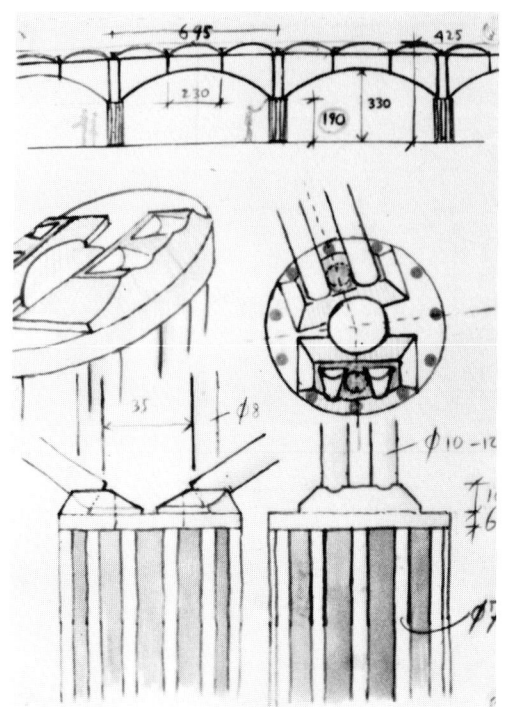

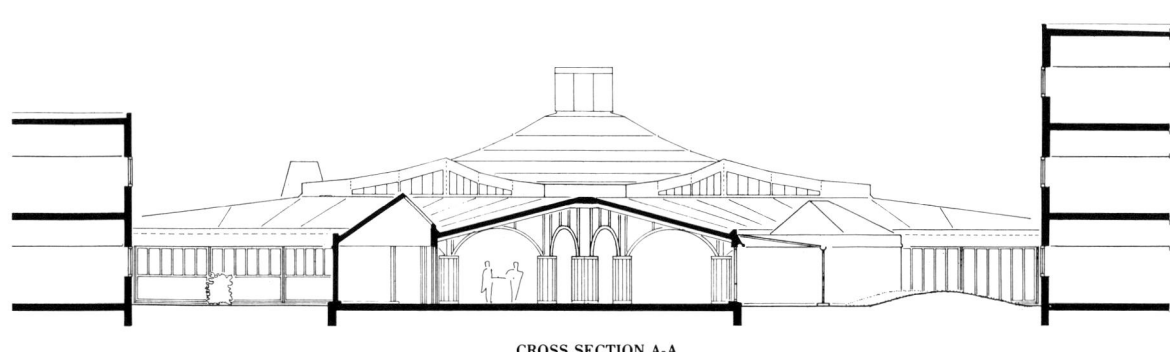

CROSS SECTION A-A

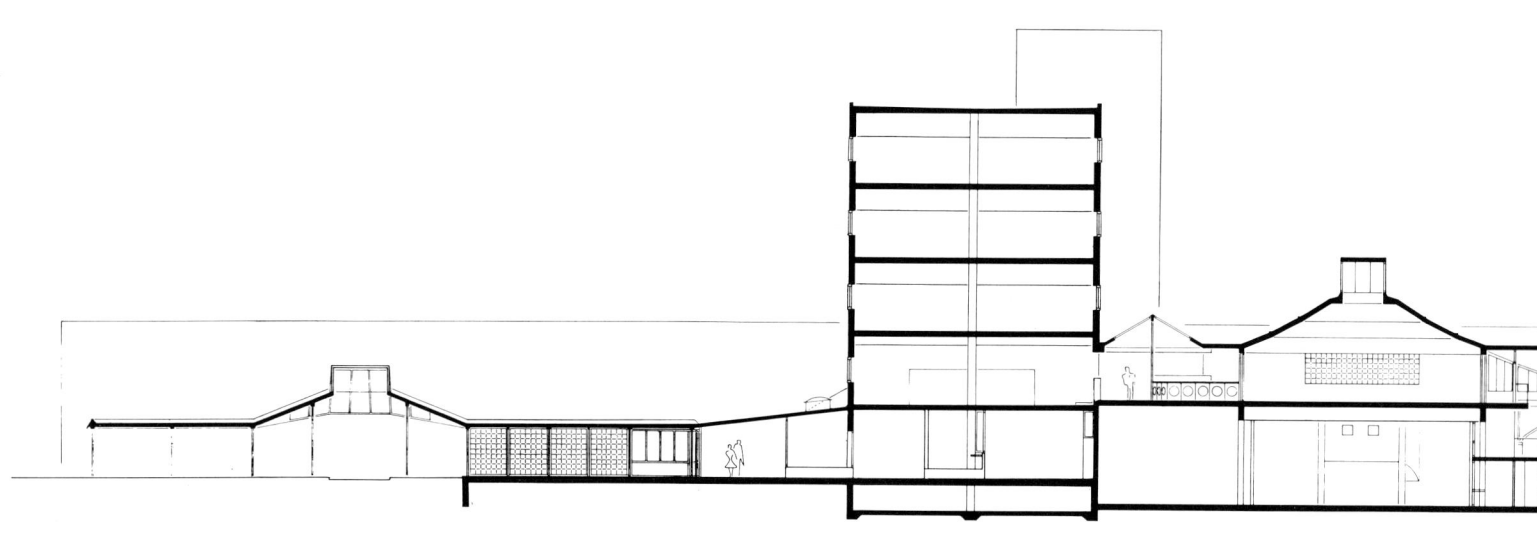

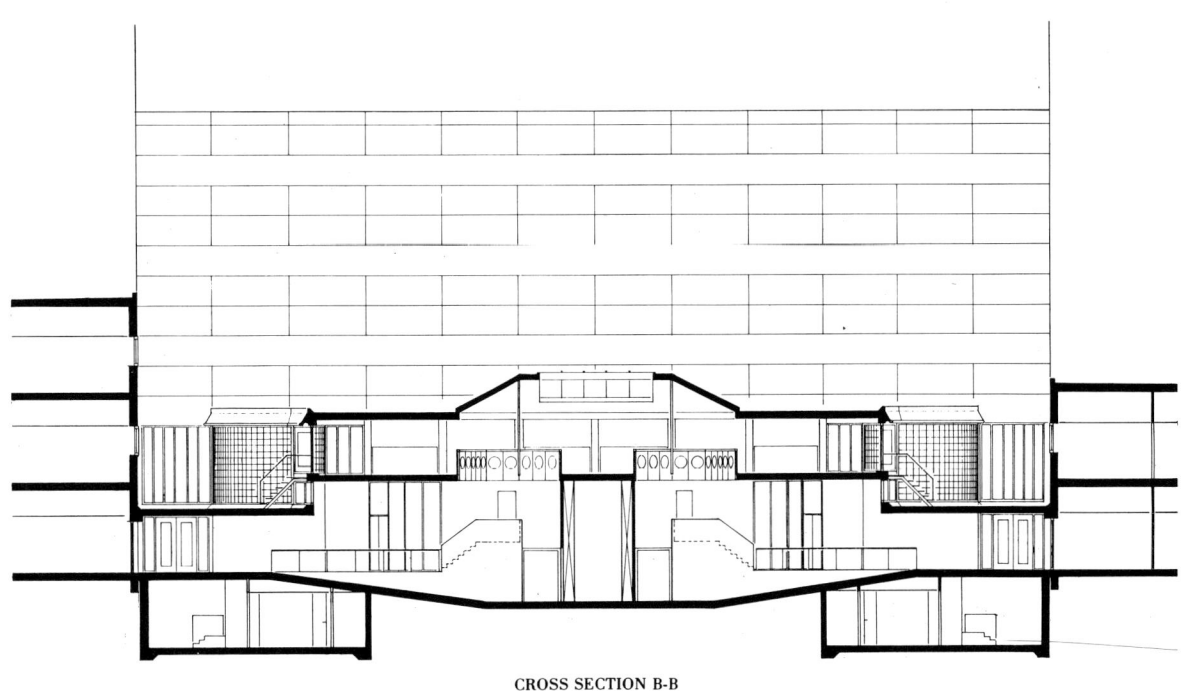

CROSS SECTION B-B

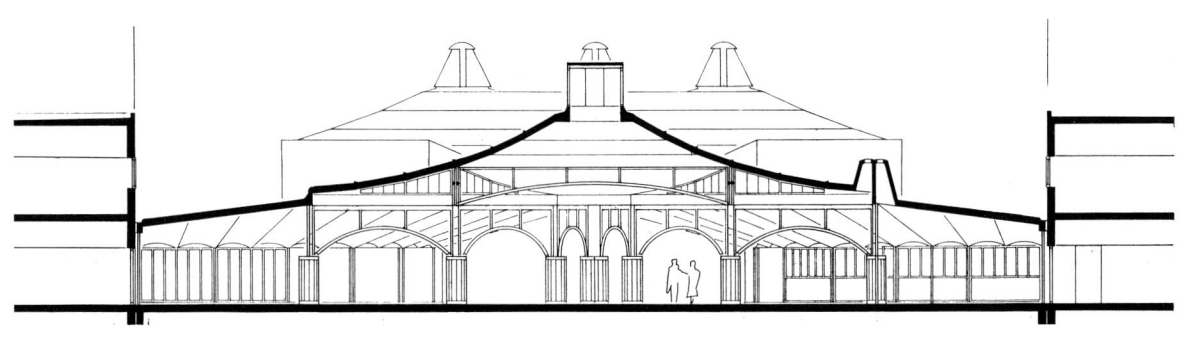

CROSS SECTION C-C

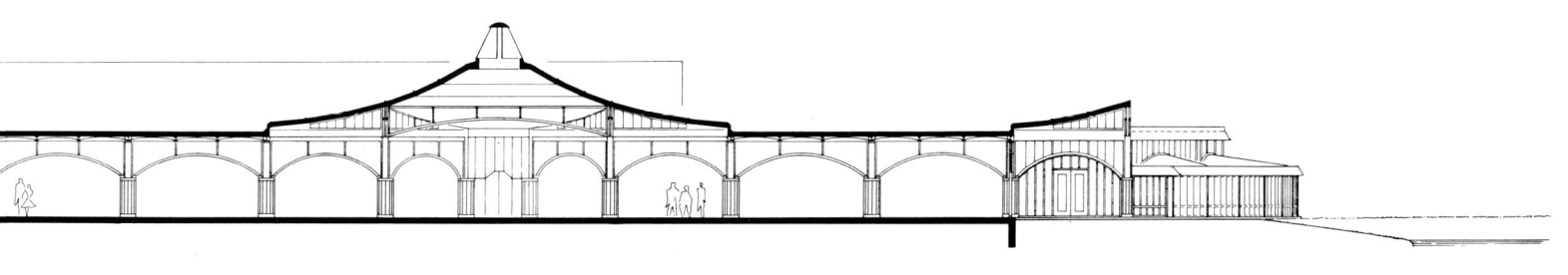

LONGITUDINAL SECTION D-D

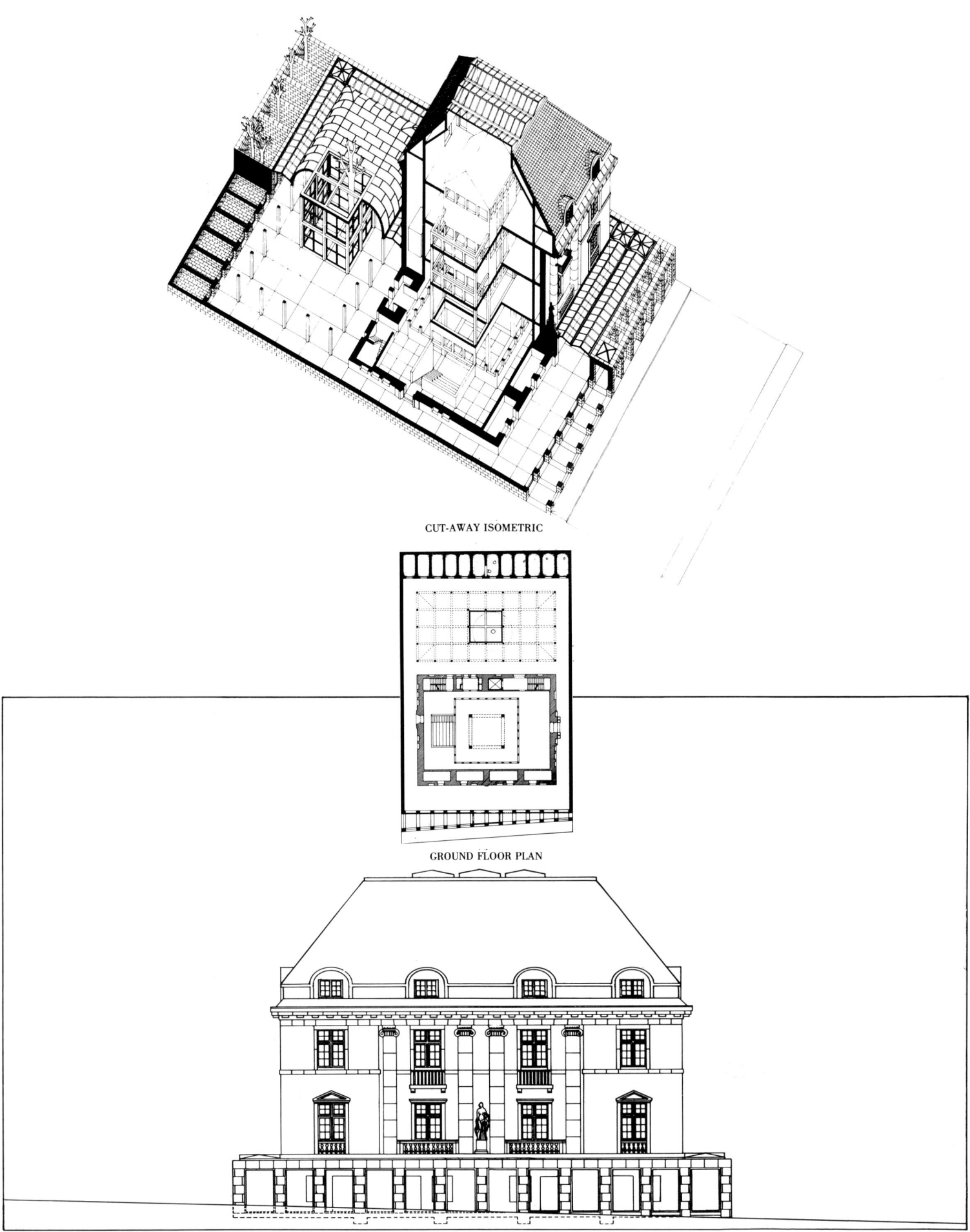

CUT-AWAY ISOMETRIC

GROUND FLOOR PLAN

NORTHWEST ELEVATION

O M UNGERS
Museum of Architecture at Frankfurt
1984

PERSPECTIVE VIEW OF THE LICHTHOF ON THE FIRST LEVEL

The Museum of Architecture is sited on the Schaumainkai in Frankfurt and is part of an overall city concept known in Frankfurt as the 'Embankment of Museums'. The plan envisages a row of museums – some new, others making use of existing buildings – along the quay. The concept of an Embankment of Museums has several notable objectives. First: the creation of a new cultural centre for the city. The Embankment of Museums revives the old humanistic concept of a spiritual and cultural forum which first took form in the 'Island of Museums' in Berlin in the nineteenth century. Second: the maintenance of a building structure that is historically appropriate to the site. This is being achieved through the fitting of functionally appropriate interiors into the existing buildings on the bank of the River Main. And third: the realisation of a decentralisation of functions. This will enable a mix of functions such as culture, services, employment and accommodation to take place both in individual places and on the whole embankment. These three objectives are keys to contemporary urban planning that should not be underestimated. They extend beyond strictly local boundaries and illustrate a trend of great importance to contemporary urban planning, regardless of where it takes place. It is in this context that one should also see the individual museum building and the overall plan.

Within the framework of the city concept described above, the museum was allocated a relatively small piece of land with an existing double villa on the corner of the Schaumainkai and Schweizerstrasse. The villa itself was not of great architectural/historical importance but was a somewhat pallid imitation of the architecture of the Biblioteca Laurenziana. But that was not important: all that mattered was the 'memory value' (*Erinnerungswert*) of the house: it had acquired value in the form of collective memories marking the place where it stood and the history of that place. This value alone was sufficient justification for preserving the house. Of course it would have been easier and – from an objective point of view – better to have built a new museum on the site of the old house. It would also have been cheaper. However, the value of the place justified the decision to preserve the house and incorporate it in a new museum concept.

There were two ways of preserving the building. One was to simply restore what was there, the other was to incorporate the substance of the old building in a new concept, making it the content and theme of the concept itself. The first option was discounted on functional grounds: the villas were not suited for use as a museum. So only the second option remained, ie, to upgrade the old building to a museum building.

How did this happen? First of all the whole site was transformed into a house or an inner room by surrounding it with a wall. By this device the old house itself stood as an object in an exhibition room, becoming at the same time an object on display as well as the medium of display. As an object it was to some extent elevated and thereby alienated but it also gained a new meaning which went far beyond the true, original purpose of the house.

The existing floor structure did not meet the new requirements, so the old house had to be gutted, leaving only the outer shell. A new structure was built into the inner room that was freed by doing this. This inner structure assumed the exhibition functions.

The resulting architectural theme was the 'house within a house'. The outer shell is a thick wall with niches, bays and hollow spaces, comparable to an old city wall. The inner shell is the profiled wall with the windows, columns, pillars, profiles and protrusions of the old house. And inside that is the archetype of a house with a dematerialised skin.

The morphological concept of the project also entails the changing of space in the sense of a never-ending sequence of inner and outer rooms. The 'room within a room' leads the visitor to an outer room then into an inner room, which is itself an outer room in relation to the next inner room and so on. It is a sequence which cannot be brought to a close. It therefore expresses continuity of both thought and feeling. The continuity of space itself is the principle of the design. The function as well as the physical restrictions of the site answer the requirements of this principle, which is based on the unification of opposites and not on their separation. Nikolaus von Kues expressed it as the *Coincidentia Oppositorium*: the coincidence of opposites which are mutually dependent and not mutually exclusive. The innermost space is an illustration: it consists of an abstract (filigree) grating through which the natural form of an established chestnut tree thrusts. This is another commentary in an extreme form on the principles of design that have been applied here. The abstract cage stands in opposition to the natural object represented by the tree. It symbolises conceptual space in opposition to natural space, but at the same time shows us how these two oppositions are inter-dependent and united in their morphological dependency. The architectonic concept is paradigmatic for the city as a whole. It must be understood as a spatial microcosm in the macrocosmic space of the city.

Collaborators: M Baum and G Sunderhaus.

Translated from the German by Pamela Johnston

JOHN HEJDUK
Three Projects
1962-66

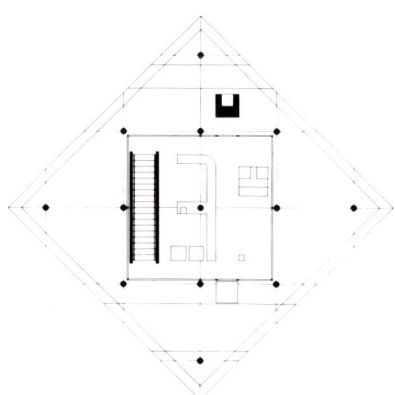

PROJECT A, HOUSE, ENTRANCE LEVEL PLAN

The following projects are the result of a search into generating principles of form and space in architecture. There is an attempt to understand certain essences in regard to an architectural commitment with the hope of expanding a vocabulary. The discovery of the workings and dictates of an organic development of specific ideas becomes a necessary function of the search. A liberation of mind and hand becomes possible which perhaps leads to certain transformations and visions of form regarding space.

The realisation that works in the Arts are the embodiment of specific plastic points of view, that the mind and hand are as one, working on primary principles, and of filling these principles through juxtaposition of basic relationships within the vocabulary of point, line, plane, volume, opened up the possibility of argumentation.

The first moves are arbitrary; but once the arbitrary beginning is committed, once the initial intuitions are experienced, it then becomes necessary that the organism proceeds through its natural evolution; and whether the evolution of form continues or stops depends upon the use of the intellect not as an academic tool but as a passionate living element.

The problems of point-line-plane-volume, the facts of square-circle-triangle, the mysteries of central-peripheral-frontal-oblique-concavity-convexity, of right angle, of perpendicular, of perspective, the comprehension of sphere-cylinder-pyramid, the questions of structure-construction-organisation, the question of scale, of position, the interest in post-lintel, wall-slab, the extent of a limited field, of an unlimited field, the meaning of plan, of section, the meaning of spatial expansion – spatial contraction – spatial compression – spatial tension, the direction of regulating lines, of grids, the forces of implied extension, the relationships of figure to ground, of number to proportion, of measurement to scale, of symmetry to asymmetry, of diamond to diagonal, the hidden forces, the ideas of configuration, the static with the dynamic, all begin to take on the form of a vocabulary.

The projects were begun not knowing all the above beforehand, but knowing that the basic orders needed to be searched for, becoming known as the work progressed, as the work was analysed, as the work was criticised, as the work was formed. In order to make principles meaningful and to have them put forth organic revelations, there had to be a given form. The arguments and points of view are within the work, within the drawings. It was hoped that the conflicts of form would lead to a clarity which could be useful and even perhaps transferable.

One of the major arguments which eventually caused the disengagement of the De Stijlists Theo van Doesburg and Piet Mondrian during the 1920s was when Van Doesburg tipped by 45° the internal right angle relationships within the canvas, thereby destroying the original internal 90° which ran parallel with the edge of the canvas (Fig 1).

This act caused a serious formal disagreement with regard to the significance of right-angle relationships in which Mondrian was actively and spiritually involved. Mondrian's answer to Van Doesburg's 45° internal relationship was to tip the canvas, but still maintain the internal right-angle 90° relationships as far as the observer was concerned (Fig 2). The formal ramifications of this action were shattering, the peripheric tensions of the edge and contours were heightened and the extension of field was implied beyond the canvas. The ideas in this point of view were not experimented with as far as the spatial implications in architecture were concerned.

The enclosed diamond projects are a first attempt to investigate the above formal possibilities in architecture. A number of problems emerge; however, before going into these, a few points as to the Cubist space translated into architecture should be made. Among other things the Cubist painters were interested in the strong centralisation of figures upon the canvas, with a decrease of activity towards the periphery of the field along with the problems of shallow depth; and the strong 90°, 60°, 30°, 45° gridings and the interlocking of planar figures. Le Corbusier was cognisant of the Cubist ideas as far as spatial problems. The Carpenter Center at

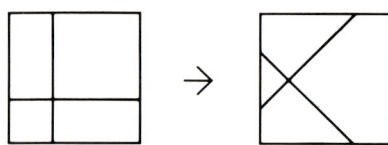
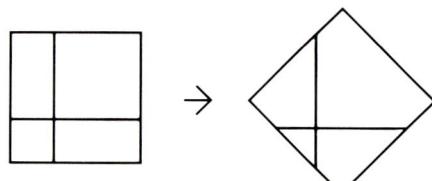
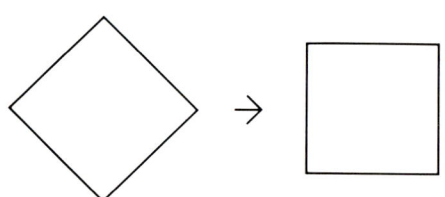

FIG 1   FIG 2   FIG 3

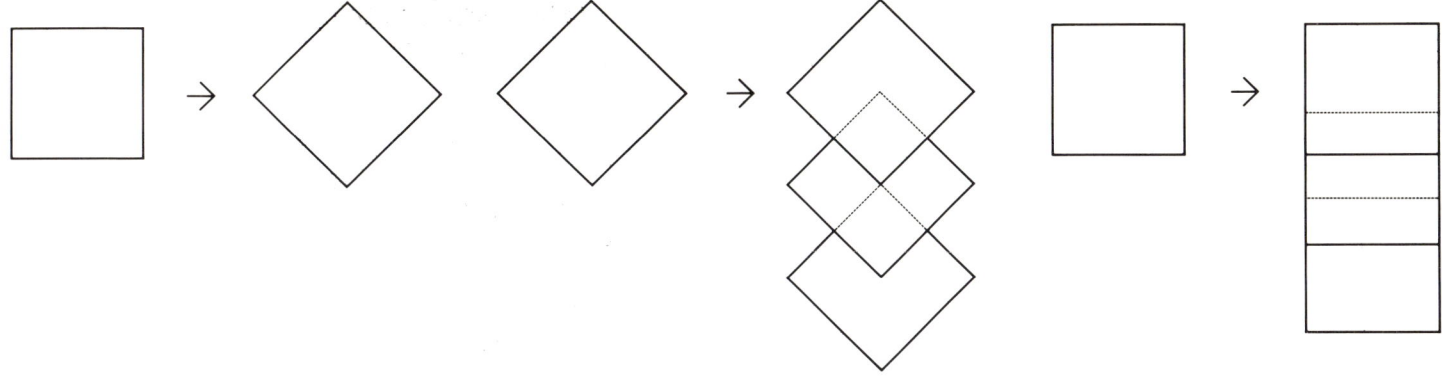

FIG 4　　　　　　　　　　　　　　　　FIG 5　　　　　　　　　　　　　　　　FIG 6

Harvard is a prime rendition of the problems of Cubist space translated into architecture. Mies van der Rohe in the Hubbe and Lange houses of the early part of the century shows equal interest in the idea of an abstract plan and the spatial matrix involved in the treatment of plan as a two-dimensional problem.

Yet Mondrian worked first as a Cubist, and then moved from Cubism into Neo-Plasticism. He continually urged architects to delve into the spatial ideas of his paintings; however, the architects of his time apparently were not interested in adopting the diamond configuration. One of the major architectural arguments of today still concerns the dialectic between the concepts of two-dimensional and three-dimensional space.

Le Corbusier's earlier buildings such as Villa Garches were magnificent conceptions of the flat two-dimensional aspect of architectural form, yet are curious because of the insistence of a single preferred point of view, that is, the facade presented as a flat composition to the eye of the observer very much like the plans. There is in the elevation a recall of the Renaissance vision of external form, the problem of composing upon a two-dimensional surface.

The uniqueness of architecture does not lie only in the presenting of a perfectly flat facade or in the creation of an elaborate volumetric building spiralling in oblique exaggerated deep perspectives.

If the Cubist canvas provided thought to the architects of the twenties, there may be some significance in the diamond canvases of Mondrian for architects of today. The initial spatial evolution in the form of a new *projected* and *exploded* space and the spatial implications are sought after in the Diamond projects. Another way of looking at space and form can be adopted. The Renaissance space of perspective is a fact; the flat-shallow contained-flux space of the post-Cubist canvas is a fact.

When a diamond form in plan is projected by isometric it becomes a square (Fig 3). This may appear to be a self-evident truth, but such projections, that is, the projections of diamond forms into isometrics, had not appeared in architectural drawings prior to these explorations. The converse has been in existence and use, that is, the square drawn in isometric which becomes a diamond (Fig 4).

When a square form in plan is drawn in isometric it appears to the eye as a three-dimensional projection. When more than one floor plan is projected in isometric, it builds up quite naturally and still appears as a three-dimensional representation (Fig 5). When the diamond is drawn in isometric and has a plan of more than one floor, a very special phenomenon occurs (Fig 6). The forms appear two-dimensional; the storeys overlap each other in a primary two-dimensional vision. The forms tip forward in isometric towards the picture plane; they are three-dimensional, yet a stronger reading of two-dimensionality predominates. A meshing together of two dimensions pushing forward is the phenomenon we are most aware of.

As the Cubists in their paintings tipped objects forward towards the picture plane, the isometric projections of the diamond accomplished a similar point of view for architectural drawings. The isometric projections of the diamond are Cubist projections in architecture, therefore, completing the formal relationship between Cubist projection in painting and Cubist projection in architecture.

The quality of space is transferred to the observer in the diamond isometrics without using the antique and outmoded form of perspective projection. The two-dimensionality of a plan, projected into the three-dimensional isometric, still appears two-dimensional, closer to the two-dimensional abstraction of the plan and perhaps closer to the actual two-dimensionality of the architectural space.

With regard to the actual three-dimensional space of the diamond configuration, certain problems arise and bring forth an aspect of encompassing lateral extension and vision. The presentation of a flat two-dimensional surface and facade is not unique; it implies frontality and a single point of view. Perhaps the history of space in architecture can be represented by Figure 7, in which 'a' denotes the past, 'b', the present and 'c,' the future.

Futures can only be speculated upon. When the observer is external to the diamond looking at the outside of the apex (Fig 8), there is a tendency of the two sides to come forward and flatten out; an extended perspective of lateral extension and vision is produced. Internally (Fig 9), the observer is confronted with a very similar phenomenon although it is the internalisation of the situation; he is again encompassed by the flattening out of the two sides; we have here the appearance of a coordination of external and internal experience. Of prime importance are the right-angle relationships of the intersections; a curvilinear surface would have the effect of softening the experience and impact. Tensions come from the opposition of straight lines, verticals and horizontals which Mondrian carefully points out in his discussions upon painting; the circle becomes somewhat suspect, but not entirely; contradictions sometimes are necessary.

The introduction of the right angle within the diamond field permits the possibility of the observer to begin the trek of the diamond confronted with continual expanding encompassation. The conclusion permits the thesis of maximum extension from the maximum compression; that of seeing space perpendicular to the observer's vision; that is, of seeing the hypothenuse laterally. The above is a somewhat compressed discussion for the admission of the diamond configuration into the family of architectural space generators.

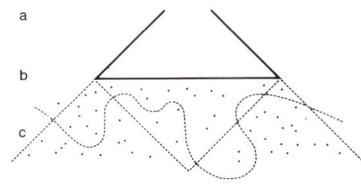

FIG 7

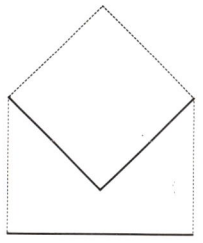

FIG 8

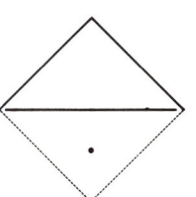

FIG 9

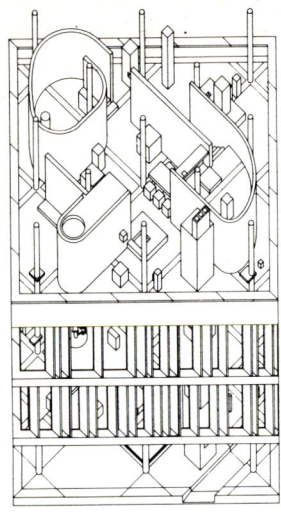

FOURTH LEVEL PROJECTION

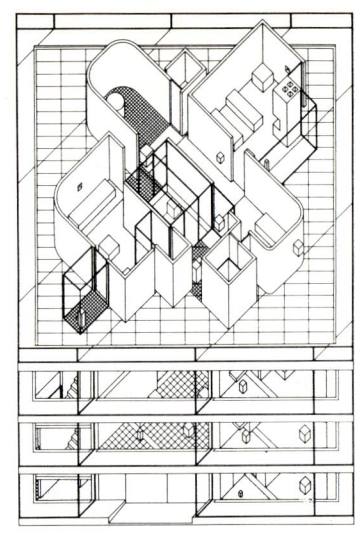

FOURTH LEVEL PROJECTION

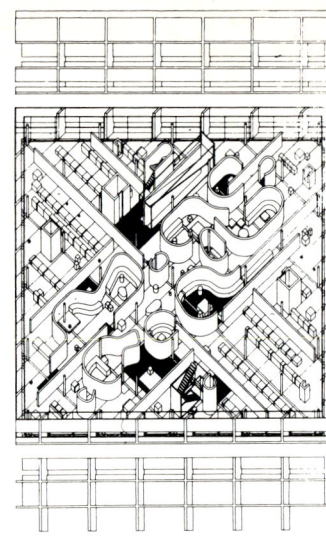

PROJECTION

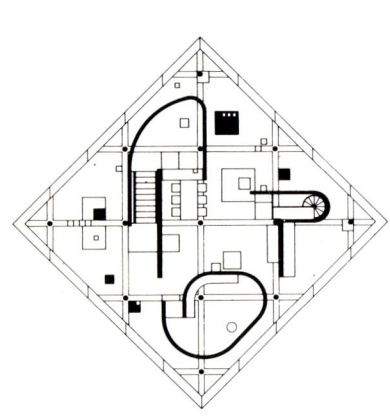

FOURTH LEVEL PLAN

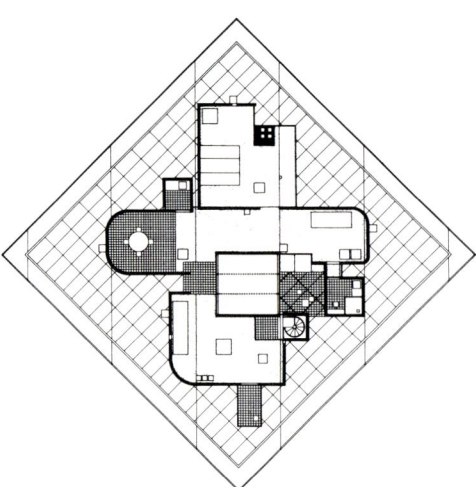

FOURTH LEVEL PLAN

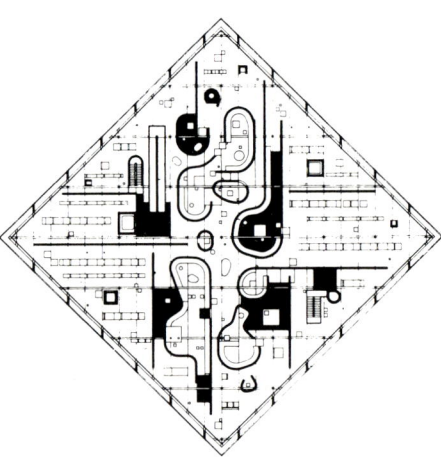

FLOOR PLAN

Project A, House
The columns, beams, and slabs are poured in place-reinforced concrete. The column grid is 13'-0" on centre and the floor-to-floor height is 10'-0".

The structural elements, columns, beams and slabs are grey. The self-supporting elements are white. The horizontal surfaces are coloured in primaries ranging from blue, red, yellow, to white. The horizontal surfaces over eye level in each space are white. All the vertical non-supporting surfaces are white, the exception being the peripheric mullion-fins.

Project B, House
The walls, beams, and slabs are poured in place-reinforced concrete. The wall grid is 17'-0" on centre and the floor-to-floor height is 11'-0".

The structural elements, slabs, and beams are grey. The structural elements of walls are white. The self-supporting panel elements are blue and red. The horizontal surfaces are coloured in primaries ranging from blue, red and yellow to white. The horizontal surfaces over eye level in each space are white.

Project C, Museum
The columns, girders, beams and slabs are poured in place-reinforced concrete. The column grid is 30'-0" on centre and the floor-to-floor height is 15'-0".

Explored within the Museum Project and within a Diamond Field are the problems of spatial compression and spatial tension; the interaction of curvilinear volumes, compressing the centre of the space, which then explodes into taut planes moving towards the periphery of the exhibition space; all played within the frame. Sculpture would be exhibited in and about the curved walls and volumes. Paintings would be exhibited on the straight extended walls.